Cultivating Radiance

Develop Your Inner Light and
Live a More Joyful Life

Cultivating Radiance

---

5 Essential Elements for Holistic Self-Care

Tamara Gerlach

Wild Oak Press
P.O. Box 30113
Walnut Creek, CA 94598
(925) 864-2093
tam@tamaragerlach.com
TamaraGerlach.com

Contents

Dedication ix
Acknowledgments xi
Introduction xiii

Element I: Beliefs 1

  1 I'll See it When I Believe It 3
  2 The Radiance of Self-Acceptance 7
  3 Appreciating Your Radiance Super-Powers 11
  4 Plugging into Source: Connection with Your Radiant Nature 15
  5 The Empowerment of Possibilities 17
  6 Creating Space for Radiance by Exposing Limiting Beliefs 19
  7 Letting Go of What Dims Our Light 23
  8 Finding "Center" 27
  9 Faucets and Drains 31
  10 Enough 33
  11 Our Global Family 37

Element II: Optimistic Attitude 41

  12 Living with an Outrageously Optimistic Attitude 43
  13 Cultivating Playfulness 45
  14 If You See Someone Without a Smile, Give Him Yours 49

15 Be a "Yes" Person 51

16 "I Love It" 55

17 Life Is Good and Keeps Getting Better: Living with Gratitude and Appreciation 59

18 Using Obstacles as a Springboard 63

19 Well, Excuse Me 69

20 Delight in Change 71

21 Practicing Infinite Patience 73

Element III: Passion **77**

22 Cultivating Passion: Passion in Action 79

23 Dream Big! 83

24 Radiant Inspiration Is Everywhere 87

25 NGU(Never Give Up) 89

26 The Passion of Adventure 93

27 Living with an Open Heart 97

28 The Passion of Our Life Purpose 101

Element IV: Self-Care Alignment **105**

29 Foundation for Radiant Alignment 107

Physical Alignment:

30 Taking Care of Our Radiant Body 111

31 Radiant Nutrition 115

32 Honoring Our Environment 119

Mental Alignment:

33 Being Fully Present 123

34 Inspirational Input 127

35 Become an Olympic Learner 131

36 Taking Mental Break Days 135

Spiritual Alignment:

37 Giving 139

38 The Energy of Breath...143
39 Clarity Through Meditation...147

Element V: Vision..**151**

40 Radiance Vision...153
41 Setting Intentions...155
42 The Non-Negotiables...159
43 Innovation and Creativity...161
44 Choreographing Your Radiance Plan............................165
45 Creating Your Team:
Who Will You Invite to the Party?................................171
46 A Radiant Front Row..175

Conclusion..**177**
Radiance Wheel..**178**
R.A.D.I.A.N.C.E..**183**
Radiance Is..**184**

Resources...**185**
About the Author..**187**

Dedication

*I dedicate this book to my partner, Ron,
whose support and love inspire me beyond measure.
I appreciate you.*

Acknowledgments

There are so many wonderful, radiant people in my life that I can only begin to acknowledge the people who inspired, mentored, and shared their knowledge with me. First, my family. I chose my parents well. Ken and Gay, you have always believed in me and encouraged me to be an intuitive entrepreneur and to follow my heart. Ron, the love of my life, thank you for loving me exactly as I am, growing with me, and creating a relationship beyond my wildest dreams. You taught me what it means to live a truly radiant life. My children, Sierra and Kyle, being your mother has been the most rewarding part of my life. You are kind and wise. And my sister, Tifany, you are an awesome mother and sister, and you have always made me laugh.

To my dear friend and editor, Julie Southern, without your talent and willingness to share your gifts, I could not have done this. Thank you for over a decade of support and friendship.

Thank you to Rich Fettke for being my life and business coach since 1998, for stretching and challenging me, and for believing in me when I didn't believe in myself.

Although I am the one who organized this book into a format that is useful for the cultivation of your radiance, I have had the honor of working with wonderful coaches and mentors, and the benefit of learning from the works of business, psychology, and spiritual leaders, and I have asked for input from some of the most radiant people on the planet. I owe so much to all of the radiant people who agreed to be interviewed.

Thank you to Ron Abram, Sierra Dasso, Jan Heise, Trish Peterson, Francine Allaire, Wes Hopper, Kimber Simpkins, Kristine Carlson, Kathy Fettke, Patrick Ryan, Mai Vu, Rich Fettke, Jolie Keyser, Virginia Kelley, Dennis Miu, Greg Riley, Suzanne Sutton, Mike Lynch, Lisa Elfstrum, Steve Zodtner, Stefanie Baeker, David Allen, Andrea Schmid, Alison Marks, Nicole Forzano, Elaine Jaynes, Bart Hawkins, Stig Mogensen, Sis Morris, and Barbara Fester for sharing your wisdom. All of you are delightfully sprinkled throughout this book.

A special thank you to the venerable Master Jian Sheng and the Shifu at Buddha Gate Monastery for years of teaching me through example what it means to be kind, compassionate, patient, and graceful. You are truly radiant.

A warm thank you to my new friends, Donna Kozik, for being a great writing coach and sharing your resources, and to Lisa Keating, for your excellent photography.

And, to all of my clients over the years, you have taught me so much through your courage, authenticity, and growth. Thank you for trusting me with your life.

Introduction

Not long ago, there was a beautiful and daring young child named Grace, who loved to explore, play, and use her imagination dreaming of special friends and far away places. This child's eyes were bright and delightful, with a light that illuminated the world, and her laughter and joy inspired all of the people around her. Everybody loved Grace. Of course; why wouldn't they? She was a magnificent child.

As Grace grew older, people would say things like "stop daydreaming," "get serious," or "no, you're doing it wrong." Even though she resisted it at first, little by little, her light grew dimmer.

Then one day Grace became a teenager. People would say "you don't look right," "you don't fit in," or "you're not good enough," and Grace began to believe them because suddenly things didn't feel right, so she started to separate herself from the other kids. She felt as though everyone else was on the boat, but she was in the water and didn't even deserve to climb aboard. She began to doubt if her life mattered. What Grace didn't realize is that everyone else felt as though they were in the water, too.

Her light grew dimmer…

…and dimmer, through several failed relationships and unfulfilling jobs. The voices of self-doubt and self-criticism seemed to be omnipresent, and exhaustion was the standard. Grace always felt like she should be doing it all and that she never did enough, which robbed her of energy and confidence.

This went on for way too many years, until one day the now grown-up, weary, but hopeful Grace decided it was time to change her story. She wanted to reconnect with the joy and light that came so easily as a child. She wanted to believe in possibilities again, and have passion and purpose. Grace wanted to be alive.

And so, our daring and magnificent Grace, began the journey of self discovery and cultivating radiance.

As my outside ages, my intention is to become stunningly beautiful on the inside.

What does "cultivating radiance" mean?

Cultivating is to develop or improve by education or training; to refine; to promote the growth or development of; to devote oneself to.

Radiance is brightness or light; warm, cheerful brightness. It is the light that passes through, is emitted by, or reflected from you.

So, cultivating radiance is developing your inner light.

Why Cultivate Radiance? If you are a bright, cheerful person who has positive beliefs and attitudes and lives in alignment, and with passion, you will have a more fulfilling life, healthy relationships, and you will be "in the flow". You will be "on the boat"...with all the Radiant people.

This book was born out of a self-care strategic plan that I had been using with my life- and business-coaching clients for many years. It seemed that there were so many brilliant people with great potential who were stuck, lacked confidence, or were just plain exhausted. Their light had dimmed. The self-care plan helped them come back to life, and I sensed there were more like them who needed this information.

There were also certain people in my life who really stood out as radiant, living their lives fully present, and with happiness and joy as their foundation. I set out on a journey to learn their secrets. I discovered that while what they do is very similar, how they do it varies dramatically, from meditation to regular adrenaline rushes.

We will focus on the what and the why. I will give examples, stories, discovery questions, and activities to help you to create your own personal how based on your life and what works for you. As I went through months of interviews with these radiant souls, I began to implement what I learned and discovered that this stuff really works! I am giddy about sharing it with you.

We all have access to unlimited radiance. Know that *all* radiant people have suffered disappointment, made mistakes, hurt others, cried (usually a lot), been stressed, and felt depression and fear, but they learned to appreciate the lessons and never give up on themselves or their dreams.

Mindful cultivation of radiance is a sensual practice. In your mind, see and feel yourself as a radiant person – not as a person who may have lost her radiance in certain parts of her life, but as someone who already has it, and is turning it up and making that light even brighter. See yourself as radiant, then create it. You are all that and so much more.

Each chapter is designed to take you on a journey to discovering your Radiant Nature. They often begin with a quote to get you warmed up. Next, the body to inspire ideas and possibilities. Then, you will answer a "discovery question". This is to help you deepen the learning and bring it into your own life. The "activities" are designed to help you get into action around the learning, to challenge and stretch you. After that, there is a "gratitude" piece because gratitude is so foundational to Radiance that it is important to include it into every chapter. Lastly, there is a "mantra" or mind tool ("man" means "mind", and "tra" means "tool" in Sanskrit); it is a way to consistently send ourselves positive thoughts and create momentum in our intended direction. Saying the mantras is not enough, you must feel them in your heart and believe them in your mind in order to have an impact on your life. So, if the mantras do not resonate with you, choose others that do.

It is a good idea to have a journal or notebook as you go

through the chapters to help you focus, to bring a deeper level of learning, and to allow you to manifest your ideas from your mind onto paper and into reality.

As you go through the chapters, reading, answering the discovery questions, doing the activities, and repeating the mantras, you will learn to turn on all of your senses and really experience your own Radiance in a very physical, mental, and spiritual way, awakening what makes you come alive to a fulfilling, joyous life.

You will recover your natural alignment and inner light as you increase happiness by expanding your freedom from obstacles, exploring possibilities and choices, and steping into your Radiant essence, connection to Source, and oneness with all.

An advantage to cultivating your own radiance is that you not only create your own spectacular life, but you get to share it with the world. Everyone benefits.

The light is always there; sometimes it just needs a little cultivation.

Be mindful to take each bite slowly. Read a chapter, then let the learning sink into every cell of your body and do its magic.

An important skill is to keep asking yourself "why" or "what" at every step of your journey. Why do I want to be radiant? Why do I want to deepen my understanding or compassion? What do I want to gain from doing these things? What will I do with more radiance in my life?

As you begin to change, ask: How does it feel to be more radiant? What changes do I see?

When you change your energy in any situation, the energy of everything around you also changes, especially if it is the way you think or feel about something. Discover your "what" and "why," and the "how" will come naturally.

Invoke Your Radiance Super-Powers

All superheroes are able to connect with their power and get into action to save the day. Your super-power is your light. Get into your proverbial phone booth and come out dressed and ready to take on the world.

We cannot think our way into radiance; we must begin to *act* differently. When you are hungry, you could think about food, but it would be much more beneficial for you to actually eat it. So it goes with the exercises in this book. It will not benefit you to look at each section and then just think about it. Don't think about how nice it would be to take care of yourself, or how you would like to someday implement some of these concepts. *Do it!* Do it now. Begin to create habits that will last for the rest of your life. *You are too important* to let another day go by without fully honoring your self, your health, and your connection to the rest of us. We need you – *all* of you.

The sections include the five essential elements: beliefs, optimistic attitude, passion, self-care alignment, and vision.

Creating your personal radiance plan will bring you into the flow of balancing your inner self with what is going on around you. The good news is that *you* are the expert on yourself, and you *know* what you need to be in alignment. You are able to take care of yourself with ease and grace, create serenity without guilt or force, and become empowered. Please don't take my word for it; take what you like from this book and discover for yourself what cultivating radiance is about.

Element 1:
Beliefs

---

*"If you don't have solid beliefs
you cannot build a stable life.
Beliefs are like the foundation of a building,
and they are the foundation to
build your life upon."
~ Alfred A. Monatpert*

I'll See it When I Believe It

"I understand that what I believe to be absolutely true becomes true because I believe it."

~ *Patrick J. Ryan*

Our beliefs are so powerful that as we become aware of or change what we believe, what we see begins to align with it. Since so many of our beliefs are unconscious and habitual, our challenge is to create awareness of what motivates our behaviors. The things that consistently show up in our lives that we seemingly do not want usually have an unconscious belief.

There once was a wise sage who lived along the path at the edge of a village. One day a traveler was on his way to the village and stopped to visit the sage.

"I have never been to this village. Can you tell me about the people here?" asked the traveler.

The sage said, "Sure, but first tell me about the people in the village you came from."

"Oh, they are terrible, rude, and unfriendly, and cannot be trusted. That is why I left."

The sage said, "Well, I have bad news for you. The people here are exactly the same"

Later that day, another traveler was heading to the village and stopped to visit the sage.

"I have never been to this village. Can you please tell me about the people here?" asked the traveler

The sage said, "Sure, but first tell me about the people in the village you came from."

"Oh, they are wonderful, kind, loving, and generous," replied the traveler.

The sage said, "Well, I have good news for you. The people here are exactly the same."

Assuming that the first traveler consciously truly did want to be happy and connected to cool people, his unconscious beliefs kept him from achieving it. He could go from village to village and always find the same thing. In just the same way, people can go from job to job, or relationship to relationship, and keep finding the same things. The world is full of our mirrors, reflecting back to us what we are giving.

We create our environment through our beliefs. If you want to know about your past, look at what is happening in your present. If you want to know about your future, look at what you are doing in the present. What messages have you been unconsciously sending? What beliefs are behind those messages?

Until we believe in ourselves, we undermine everyone else's belief in us. It is our responsibility to set the foundation of our own life.

Our mind does not know whether our beliefs are "real" or not, so our body reacts physically to our beliefs. As a child we believed many things that felt very real to us. We could've "sworn" by them – beliefs such as Santa Claus or that our teachers live at school. As we get older, our beliefs change as we collect evidence that tells us differently.

What we believe affects how we behave. Let go of self-limiting beliefs and, like the second traveler, tell the story of ease and delight. Believe that you can change every aspect of your life to create more radiance. Believe that you are fabulous and radiant, and everything around your will mirror it!

Discovery Question:
What positive beliefs about myself serve me well? Why?

Activity:
Sit comfortably and take some long, deep breaths. Get in touch with your body, and become aware of your energy. Then ask yourself: How radiant am I? Where could I cultivate my beliefs?

Gratitude:
Appreciate the people who have taught you the most about believing in yourself and the world around you.

Mantra:
I see the world as radiant.

The Radiance of Self-Acceptance

"The secret of attraction is to love yourself. Attractive people judge neither themselves nor others. They are open to gestures of love. They think about love, and express their love in every action. They know that love is not a mere sentiment, but the ultimate truth at the heart of the universe."

~ Deepak Chopra

Embrace who you are right now, rather than who you think you "should" be. It does not mean that we stop being motivated to grow, but we are content with where we are in the process. When we honestly look at ourselves without judgment or criticism, we realize that we're not bad, and we do our best with what we've got at the time. Self-acceptance opens us to receive the beauty and adventure life has to offer.

Acceptance is such a beautiful thing that allows us to be at peace with what is and even embrace those things that seemingly block our way. Embrace your age and your body. It is a fact of life that our body ages, everything changes, and, like we read at the beginning of the book, we can become more stunningly beautiful on the inside. Our insides show on our outside.

There is a wonderful video called "Jessica's Daily Affirmation" where an adorable little girl named Jessica very enthusiastically dances and performs as she recites a litany of all the things she likes. She likes her dad, mom, aunts, cousins, hair, room, and whole house. Then she runs off, yelling "I can do anything!" She joyfully accepts everything in her life. It was so easy when we were 5 years old. Let's get back to that place where we accept ourselves for who we are, because we are cool, we like ourselves, and we can do anything.

There is a big difference between tolerance and acceptance. We tolerate our own attachment to what our false ego thinks something ought to be, but in fact is not. Imagine saying to someone "I tolerate you," as opposed to "I accept you." Nobody wants to feel tolerated; we want to be accepted for who we are.

Acceptance gives us the ability to recognize that we are infinitely empowered to do whatever it takes to overcome any situation. It gives us the foundation to deal with any perceived problem, whether it concerns relationship, money, work, or whatever. All we need to do is accept ourselves as we are.

Believing that you deserve good in your life will open the door to an abundant flow of radiance.

When we accept ourselves, we can stop treating ourselves like a rented mule. When we stop self-abuse, acting like a victim, or maintaining other negative beliefs, we then have space to create what we want in our life. We learn to truly accept ourselves as we are. This may take practice, especially if we have spent years criticizing ourselves.

When you look in the mirror, notice if it is covered with the "dust of delusion" – those thoughts that keep us from seeing our radiance. Then get out your cloth and remove the dust so you can see your true reflection.

"To say something nice about yourself, this is the hardest thing in the world for people to do. They'd rather take their clothes off."

~ Nancy Friday

Dance a life force through you. Dance with what you want to embrace, whether it is jealousy, shame, abundance, or joy. Feel it in you and let it move you. Let go of old, lower vibrations to make space for radiance.

We can learn to accept and embrace our duality; we all have feminine and masculine power, intellect and intuition, light and dark, and joy and suffering. With acceptance of ourselves we integrate all of our parts to create our radiance. It is when we are at odds with or fight against certain parts of us that we get out of alignment.

Accept yourself even when dealing with some of the things our culture does not typically see as radiant, like fear, doubt, or shame. We can go to the core of the feeling and love it. Be willing to sit with your shame for as long as it takes to communicate its message. Do not resist or release it; just hear it. What is it saying? What lesson does it offer? Validate and love *all* parts of you.

This unconditional love for yourself allows you to be with anything and turn it into light. Magically, when we accept all of our parts, the ones that used to get in our way lose their power.

> An elderly farm woman had two large pots. Each hung on the ends of a pole, which she carried across her neck. One of the pots had a crack in it, while the other pot was perfect and always delivered a full portion of water.
>
> At the end of the long walks from the stream to the house, the cracked pot arrived only half-full. For a full two years this went on daily, with the woman bringing home only one and a half pots of water.
>
> Of course, the perfect pot was proud of its accomplishments. But the poor cracked pot was ashamed of its own imperfection, and miserable that it could only do half of what it had been made to do.

After two years of what it perceived to be bitter failure, it spoke to the woman one day by the stream.

"I am ashamed of myself, because this crack in my side causes water to leak out all the way back to your house," said the pot.

The old woman smiled. "Did you notice that there are flowers on your side of the path, but not on the other pot's side? That's because I have always known about your 'flaw,' so I planted flower seeds on your side of the path, and every day while we walk back, you water them. For two years I have been able to pick these beautiful flowers to decorate the table. Without you being just the way you are, there would not be this beauty to grace the house."

Each of us has our own unique flaws. But it's the cracks and flaws we each have that make our lives together so very interesting, rewarding, and radiant.

Discovery Question:
What would I like to accept about myself?

Activities:
- From the list of what you would like to accept about youself from the discovery question above, choose one thing per day to accept about yourself until the list is complete. Then, keep adding to it.
- Practice accepting and being grateful for any situation for what it is teaching offering you.
- Write a letter to your present self from your 90-year-old self. What might your future self tell you is important to cultivate?

Gratitude:
Show appreciation for your flaws and radiance that helps flowers bloom.

Mantra:
I love and accept myself exactly as I am.

Appreciating Your Radiance Super-Powers

"True happiness involves the full use of one's power and talents."
~ Douglas Pagels

Using our strengths and talents is a way for us to create success and be happy doing what moves our soul. Here we find alignment easily, so let's focus on our strengths! Sure, we all have "non-strengths," but why not focus on that which we are already brilliant? Focusing on our weaknesses is not a very effective way to evoke our super-powers.

As we tap into and step just a little bit further into our strengths and talents, we develop our belief in ourselves and awaken our inner radiance.

One summer I took my gymnastics staff camping. One of our staff members brought a friend along. He was a sweet young man who helped out around the gym often. Around the campfire I posed the question "What are you great at?" and one-by-one each enthusiastically answered how they were talented – until we got to him. He dropped his head and answered "nothing." Of course, we all jumped in with twenty things that *we* knew he was great at. It was so sad to learn that he truly believed he was good at nothing, and it showed in his life and his radiance, or lack thereof.

When we practice appreciating and using our strengths every

day, it gives us the foundation we will need when life gets difficult and requires us to dig deep for strength.

When we go into a new situation or have feelings of insecurity, rather than shrinking back, we can extend our gifts to others. By leading with our strengths as an offering, we share the most sacred parts of us. We lower our arrogance and give freely what we were born to do, or what talents have developed, so that we may be well used and serve the highest purpose. We contribute to the success of others.

Take a look at the list below and check off the talents and strengths that come easily and naturally to you and tap into your radiance. Another clue that it is your strength is if you do it without self-criticism. For instance, one of my strengths is being passionate. I never say to myself, "I shouldn't be so passionate" – never. Another one is beauty. I never think, "Wow. I just see too much beauty in everything." How ridiculous would that be?

Feel free to add more talents and strengths to the list!

Abundant	Determined	Inspirational	Positive
Active	Earthy	Intelligent	Present
Adventurous	Easy Going	Intense	Quirky
Artistic	Encouraging	Joyous	Reliable
Aware	Energetic	Kind	Resilient
Balanced	Entertaining	Literary	Resourceful
Beautiful	Enthusiastic	Loyal	Responsible
Brave	Focused	Magical	Sensitive
Bold	Free	Natural	Serene
Calm	Friendly	Nurturing	Spiritual
Caring	Giving	Organized	Subtle
Communicative	Goofy	Open	Supportive
Compassionate	Graceful	Passionate	Trustworthy
Confident	Grounded	Patient	Visionary
Creative	Honest	Peaceful	Witty
Curious	Humorous	Playful	
Dedicated	Insightful	Poetic	

Discovery Question:
How do I feel when I am doing what comes naturally and easily to me?

Activity:
Step more fully into your strengths. From the list choose the top three strengths that stand out as your most radiant super-powers.

Strength	How I will cultivate this strength?
1.	
2.	
3.	

Go to www.TamaraGerlach.com for a PDF worksheet.

Gratitude:
Show appreciation for your own strengths, talents, and inspiration as well as others.

Mantra:
I have all that I need and so much more.

Plugging into Source:
Connection with Your Radiant Nature

"There are too many people, and too few human beings."
~Robert Zend

We all have a source of infinite love and abundance always available to us if we are open to receive it. If you want more love in your life, know that you have a direct line to the Source of love.

What is "Source"? It looks different to different people. Some call it God, Spirit, Higher Power, Energy, Essence, or Allah; there are many names. We'll call it Source, meaning that it is the source of your radiance. Connecting with our Source is vital to creating the life that we want.

Many of us find our connection through time in nature, deep breathing, journaling, or sitting in silence. When we find what works best for us, we can plug into that infinite Source that offers an unlimited amount of energy to us all of the time. Unfortunately, there are so many people who live on 5 volts of energy when they could be living on 5 million volts. Most of us loosened our connection to Source at some point in our lives. This is our direct line to Source and how Source shows up through us. When we are connected on the inside it shows on the outside.

We're not just talking about connecting with the Source

of your radiant nature, but also about living that radiance, becoming radiance, and serving from radiance – loving, giving, and receiving from that beautiful energy.

We don't need to look for power, validation, or nurturing from the outside. We are all completely capable of empowering ourselves when we are plugged into Source.

Life coach, athlete, and mother Trish Petersen knows when she is out of alignment or disconnected, because she begins seeking nurturing from others. This tells her that she hasn't been nurturing herself. She then creates more consciousness around how she is feeling and the impact she is having, and then she intentionally and patiently moves back into flow and connection, and gains a sense of wholeness.

Our emotional state is our indicator. We can check in with how we are feeling to know whether we are connected to Source at any time.

When we are plugged into Source and connected to our radiant nature, we live with grace, passion, light, gratitude, ease, compassion, enthusiasm, and purpose. Our connection has a ripple effect and impacts everyone around us.

Discovery Question:
What helps me get connected to my radiant nature?

Activities:
- Spend at least fifteen minutes every day for one week (or longer) doing what helps you get connected to your radiant nature.
- Share your radiance by connecting with as many people as possible.

Gratitude:
Appreciate your Source and all that it has to offer.

Mantra:
I have the ability to reconnect and renew myself at any moment.

The Empowerment of Possibilities

"Our problem is not that we don't have power, so much as that we tend to not use the power we have."

~ Marianne Williamson

Radiant, successful people not only have positive beliefs, they feel empowered. When we feel stuck, or place our power outside of ourselves and pile on the blame, shame, guilt, and complaints, we turn ourselves into powerless victims, looking for someone to rescue us. We are unplugged from our radiant Source.

Simple solution: Move into a place of choice. Choose how you will connect and empower yourself. Turn on your own light bulb. Look at several possibilities and then move toward the best one.

We create energy around us, so if we sit there feeling like a victim, we are creating a bubble of "victim energy" all around us. We must *get up* and move to a new place with a new perspective, thereby shifting our beliefs and energy.

"I am where I am because I believe in all possibilities."
~ Whoopi Goldberg

We always have choice: choice to be empowered, choice to let go, choice to act or not and choice to be radiant. If we think we don't like our choices, we can always choose something different. It doesn't have to be this or that; we can create something that didn't already exist in our mind and expand our range of possible responses. Let go of any limits or fear of making the wrong choice and think *big*.

When we stop believing in possibilities, our thoughts become like gophers; eating away at our roots, undermining our strengths, and killing our dreams. Believe in your own abilities and utilize your radiance super-powers to give you what you need.

By exploring possibilities and choices, we free ourselves to create new understanding. We tap into a bigger field of energy and find answers in unlikely places developing our inner peace and power.

Discovery Questions:
- Where and when do I give away my power?
- What choices must I make to be more radiant?

Activity:
The next time you need to make a choice, play with the possibilities before you commit:
- Start in one place thinking about your situation. What is your current perspective?
- Then get up, move to the other side of the room, and think about it again. What new perspective could you choose? What else is possible?
- Next, go outside, stand on a chair or on your head – whatever it takes – to gain a fresh, new perspective.
- Create as many possibilities as you can, even if they seem outrageous. You may find a nugget of truth in there.
- Now, close your eyes and breathe, relax, and trust yourself. What choice will serve the highest purpose? Do that.

Gratitude:
Appreciate the people who have shown you what it is like to live an empowered life.

Mantra:
I always have choices.

Creating Space for Radiance by Exposing Limiting Beliefs

"Never think that you're not good enough yourself. A man should never think that. People will take you very much at your own reckoning."

~ Anthony Trollope

"I don't matter."

Growing up we are taught to "be humble," which sounds nice until we get so good at it that we are playing a very small game. At some point many of us learned about humility, began to dim our light, and somehow turned humility into self-criticism and even self-hatred.

Tara Brach, author of *Radical Acceptance*, tells a story about one of the Dalai Lama's early visits to the United States.

> The Dalai Lama joined a group of American and European Buddhist teachers and psychologists to talk about emotions and health. One of the participants asked him to talk about the suffering of self-hatred. The Dalai Lama was confused. He asked several people to explain, and was astonished to hear that self-hatred was a common experience in their work with others. He could not comprehend that people actually *hate themselves*.

The Western culture is a breeding ground for shame, feelings of failure, not belonging, and disconnection from Source. Our job as radiant beings is to realize when we have gone to this place of deluded thinking and deal with the cause. When we stop that thinking, we stop resisting our connection to Source and make space for radiance.

Question everything you think you know about yourself.

"Don't side with yourself."   ~ Bankei

Colluding with the self-critic is one of my favorite delusions. This is when our self-critic uses the truth against us by bringing up other times when we have failed or been hurt. We get caught when we start believing that voice that says "you can't do it," "you won't stick to it," or "you'll get hurt," and we reply with "you're right." Listen. Then, rather than believing or hating that voice, embrace it, thank it for attempting to maintain the status quo, and make a decision to do what serves your radiant nature.

Mai Vu is an international coach and speaker who came to the United States as a Vietnamese refugee. She had beliefs that kept her from taking care of herself that lasted into her adult life. She believed that self-care was for rich people and that she was a "boat person" who served the rich. She had to change her beliefs in order to change her life. The good news is that she has learned to overcome that thinking and has a brilliant radiance plan that includes regular yoga retreats to Bali and Mexico. She realized that cultivating her own radiance was about love. In order to love others, she first had to learn to love herself.

Most of us have not had to deal with such an extreme case, but we all manage to create beliefs that prevent us from fully taking care of ourselves and stepping into our radiance.

"I don't deserve."

Deflecting love and abundance dims your light. It can show up as some of these obstacles to connection with your Source:

- **Physically:** poor eating habits, too little exercise, over-working, materialism, and too little sleep.
- **Mentally or emotionally:** negative self-talk, doubt, undermining, putting ourselves last, fear of rejection, nervousness, anger, being dragged around by our emotions, resentments, neediness, obsession, fear of failure, procrastination, indecisiveness, feeling paralyzed, denial, complaining, blaming, shaming, guilt, and feeling victimized.
- **Spiritually:** as feeling unfulfilled, acting shy or going into hiding, feeling unloved or unlovable, wanting control, egoism, needing to be right, and feeling disconnected.

Accept that these things may exist for you, but do not give them any more power. Let go of your attachment to these forms of self-abuse, and do not let allow them to control or overpower your radiance.

What we embrace will stop controlling and limiting us. When we learn to manage our obstacles, our connection to our radiant nature is more available.

What we put our energy into will, in turn, create more of that energy. Our perspective is the first place to start. The goal is to come from a perspective free from self-judgment and delusions.

The world is a dualistic paradigm of opposites. In order to have radiance, we must also have darkness. We cannot ignore this part of us. We learn to embrace, understand, and make peace with it. We cannot deny it, but we do not need to live in the darkness. We always have a conscious choice: knowing that the darkness is there, and then choosing the light.

When we find ourselves in a cycle of self-doubt, anxiety, or self-criticism, we can detach and observe our limiting beliefs to see what has shown up, and then we can learn from them. Let your limiting beliefs actually help you to reach a new level of understanding.

Discovery Question:
What limiting beliefs keep me from living a more radiant life?

Activity:
- List of some of your limiting beliefs.
- Next to each belief, write down a radiant belief that you would like to replace it with.
- Contemplate the difference this change would make in your life.

  Example:

Limiting belief:	*Replace with:*	*What will change?*
self-doubt	confidence	I will stop undermining myself and move forward in my life.

Go to TamaraGerlach.com for a PDF worksheet.

Now, practice catching your limiting beliefs and replacing them with radiance.

Gratitude:
Be grateful for the awareness of your limiting beliefs so that they can be unearthed and brought to the light.

Mantra:
I choose to live in the light.

7

Letting Go of What Dims Our Light

"Holding a resentment is like me taking poison and waiting for you to die."

~ *Unknown*

Letting go of resentments and anger is vital to cultivating radiance. Have you ever met a radiant person who is full of anger and resentments? I didn't think so.

This means *really* letting it go, not just burying it (just in case we need it later). Buried anger comes out in subtle ways: passive-aggressive behavior, complaining, self-harm, sickness, low energy, and dysfunctional relationships. Radiant people have none of these things.

Jan Heise, Olympic coach and yoga master, releases what is not serving her by visualizing the unwanted energy being imbued into a rock, and then throwing it. When it leaves her hand, the energy is gone. (And no, you may not throw it at the person who triggered your feelings of resentment.)

Nobody has gone through life without doing or saying something that they wish they hadn't. Sometimes we need to forgive ourselves first. Let go of the guilt and disappointment in ourselves that dims our light. This opens us to acceptance, compassion, and understanding for ourselves, so we can then share it with others.

It is okay to have feelings of resentment, disappointment, or anger. Just be aware of attaching or clinging to them. Dwelling on these feelings only gives them more power and you less. Let them flow through you. We have all heard the saying "this too shall pass." I invite you to really take it to heart. Feelings are like the weather. Sometimes it is gorgeous, and sometimes it is stormy, but it's constantly changing.

Understand that everything is in constant flow and will change. Even when it *seems* like something will last forever, be conscious that it will end soon, and be present for the lesson that it offers. Nobody is given a "free pass" from suffering, but we do get to choose how quickly we will let go.

We judge in others what we need to heal in ourselves.

If we are holding resentments and anger, we need to examine why. There may be some payoff to our false ego like feeling in control, feeling needed, or being a martyr.

As soon as we become aware, we can ask ourselves: What is the next right thing to do coming from a compassionate heart?

False ego is the primary culprit in dimming our light, and letting go of our false ego can be one of the most difficult things to do.

For many years false ego was in total control of my life. As I care for and nurture my radiant nature, my false ego had become weaker and less verbal, but was still showing up regularly. One beautiful spring morning while I sat in our house in Truckee, California, I decided that it was time for a big part of my false ego to plug into my radiant source. It had lived out its purpose far too long, and it was no longer necessary or wanted the way it was. I began these steps to letting the miserable thing be at peace.

- First, identify "who" our false ego is. What traits does it have? When does it typically show up?
- Let a loving, radiant energy embrace and appreciate it for what it wants to teach us and for the "good intention" of wanting to keep us safe and separated.
- Turn it over to Source and let it go. It feels like a mother letting go of a child that is now ready to go out into the world alone, or like an empowered adult who is leaving the parent that kept her safe, but is no longer needed.

Once we identify and turn over our false ego, it may still show up, but now it is on the "no fly list": We have identified the danger of letting it on board and can choose to lead with our radiant nature.

Discovery Questions:
What does my radiant nature want me to let go of?
How will I let go when I feel resentful, judged, abandoned, or rejected?

Activity:
Follow the steps to connect false ego to Source and let it go:
- Identify,
- Acknowledge, and
- Say goodbye

Gratitude:
Appreciate the people who have taught you the most about letting go.

Affirmation:
I always have the choice to let go.

Finding "Center"

"Stay centered by accepting whatever you are doing. This is the ultimate."

~ Chuang-tzu

Often we hear about becoming centered or grounded. What does that mean?

Finding our center is essential to our self-care because this is what we align our thoughts, feelings, and actions with. Every day life gives us opportunities to get off-center; sometimes we get *way* off, becoming overwhelmed and exhausted, so knowing our center brings us back to a safe place.

According to Dave Allen, potter extraordinaire, when he is throwing clay, it is vital that he start with it centered on the wheel or it turns into a real mess. (It's true; I have personal experience with this one.) He must find the center of the clay and also the place on the wheel that will allow him to build and create. If you begin with the clay off-centered, you make a lot more work for yourself. You always end up with something, and it could be saved, but it just takes far more work than if you had started centered.

Many of us may have a loose idea of what that means for us and how we feel physically, mentally, and spiritually when we are centered. Finding your center is very liberating because, when we are aligned, we have more choices.

A gymnast on a balance beam who is aligned and centered can move in all directions. If she is a just little off, she still has the choice to make a correction, but if she gets too far off, she has no choice; she is going to fall off of the beam.

By really clarifying what our center feels like, and how to get there, we have the choice to come from a place of strength and alignment. From this place, no matter what challenges appear, we can create and serve the highest purpose.

Being centered does not mean that our lives no longer have pressure or resistance. It does mean that we can manage it better. Pressure can be a powerful tool to take us to new levels of achievement when we are centered. Imagine having the pressure of a project deadline if you are exhausted, scattered, and disconnected from Source. Then imagine what you could do with that project if you are strong, clear, and enthusiastic. (*Enthusiasm* comes from the Greek root *éntheos:* having a god within).

Once you know how to get centered, you can trust that you will feel when you are beginning to stray and can get back your personal alignment any time.

Discovery Questions:
What does center mean to me?
What helps me to feel centered?

Activity:
Find the places in yourself that feel solid, connected, aligned, and strong:
- Physically. Stand with your feet about hip-width apart and feel your energy connected to the earth. Become so connected that you feel unshakable, solid, and energized. Practice moving from this physically centered and connected place. Observe how it is different from when you are off balance.
- Mentally. Take a few minutes to slow your mind down, letting go of any to-do lists and becoming more present and aware. Then, just observe where your mind goes when your

thoughts are focused. Practice speaking from this mentally focused and centered place. Observe your words.

- Spiritually. Close your eyes and take several deep breaths. Put your attention on your heart and visualize its energy growing and expanding beyond the limits of your body. Listen to what your heart wants for you. Practice sharing your heart's center and observe the differences from when you are shut down or disconnected.

For instant alignment of all three, find a way to remind yourself to get centered: a word, thought, touch, or visual reminder that will bring you back to center. It can be anything from a deep breath, to placing your hand on your heart, or smiling.

Gratitude:
Appreciate all of the times that you have lost your center so that you could have the opportunity to find it.

Mantra:
I know my center and can align instantly.

Faucets and Drains

"What do we live for, if it is not to make life less difficult for each other?"
~ *George Eliot*

Some people and things are faucets, and some are drains.

In order to cultivate our radiance we must fill our energy bucket. Imagine that our energy reserves are a bucket of water, and we have access to a faucet with an infinite supply to continuously fill it. Of course first we must turn on the faucet, to allow and receive the energy, and we need to be aware of any holes we may have in our bucket. Different from the "cracked pot" story in the Radiance of Self-Acceptance chapter, these holes include: worry, self-doubt, a negative attitude, and people who do not support us, and they drain our bucket. Depending upon the number and size of the holes, our bucket may be almost empty. By patching any holes and opening the faucet, we will have more than we need and plenty to share.

When we have an understanding of what drains us, there is just one thing to do: *Stop it!*

If you put your hand onto a red-hot stove, what is your reaction? You immediately withdraw your hand. Nobody has to tell me to take your hand off. The same is true for the care of our energy reserves. When we feel pain, be it physical, mental, or spiritual, we owe it to ourselves to stop whatever is causing it. The law of cause and effect assures that we will continue to hurt ourselves until we do something different. We must change or let go of what drains us in order to reach our full potential.

Take a look at the people that fill our buckets.

Jim Rohn says, "You are the average of the 5 people you spend the most time with." It is important to average up and spend most of our time with people who help us to create radiant energy.

People who give us energy often are not only good listeners, but they tell great stories or make us laugh. We tend to be drawn to people who we feel comfortable to be ourselves around. Maybe it is a person who stretches our "comfort zone" or wakes a part of us that had been sleeping.

We all benefit from kind, trusting, open, and supportive relationships. The partners and friends that we choose become our teachers and our students. We hold up the mirror for each other, and we challenge and encourage each other. Choose your people wisely. Are they faucets or are they drains?

"Be a fountain, not a drain."   *~Rex Hudler*

Discovery Questions:
What drains me?
What gives me life, inspiration, energy, or motivation?
What does a healthy relationship look like?

Activities:
- Write down the five things that bring you to a higher level of radiance, and why they do. Start doing more of these things.
- Write down the five relationships that bring you to a higher level of radiance, and why they do. Start spending more time with these people.

Gratitude:
Appreciate someone who or something that fills your bucket.

Mantra:
I will turn on the faucet any time I need energy.

Enough

"He who knows that enough is enough will always have enough."

~ Laozi

What is enough?

Some of us have set such high standards for ourselves and others that we are setting ourselves up for disappointment and to *never* be enough. I remember being 23 years old; I owned my first business, owned my home, was married and pregnant, and was a regional director and a national team coach for USA Gymnastics, but still I never felt like I measured up. From the outside I was successful by all accounts, but on the inside I felt like I needed to be doing so much more. My belief that I was not enough left me unfulfilled and empty, searching for what I lacked.

Many of us spend our lives searching for the elusive "enough" when what we need is a new perspective. We must learn to appreciate ourselves for what we do, enjoy the fruits of our labor, and create positive energy rather than beating ourselves up for not doing or being enough, because such thinking drains our emotional energy and sucks the joy from our lives. We start by changing what we believe to be enough, and empowering ourselves to make choices and boundaries based on our own inner wisdom of what is best for our lives.

A fun way to help us find enough is to play the Goldilocks game: It's too much. It's not enough. It's just right. When we bake bread we would not pull it out of the oven before it is cooked. Nor would we leave it in the oven until it looks like charcoal. Neither extreme is of any value to us.

Sometimes enough is clear because you'll begin to feel physical or emotional pain. For example, it is apparent when we have gone beyond enough sun, enough food, or enough giving. On the other hand, sometimes we know when we have enough because we feel abundant, fulfilled, and joyful.

When we find ourselves in any situation, relationship, or decision we can play the Goldilocks game to find the balance of what feels "right." Just keep in mind that it's a game and supposed to be fun, and it's always changing, so don't get too attached to any "right" answer. We may find enough in any given moment, depending on how full our energy bucket is or what we are inspired by.

The Goldilocks game is also great for setting boundaries. For example, at work look at how much work is too much and what is too little, and then dance in the middle. Sixty hours may be too many, and ten hours are too few. Find what feels good and satisfies your lifestyle. At certain times of the year our perspective on enough will fluctuate so go with the flow.

Discovery Question:
How do I know when I have done enough?

Activities:
- Write a quick abundance list of five things that you have enough of.
- You can apply the "enough" concept to many aspects of life. Play with the possibilities in areas of your life where you would like to find enough.

  For example:
  How much is enough money? What do I need to feel secure and be able to do what I want in my life?
  What is enough time? What do I want to accomplish, and will I devote enough time to each activity?

What is enough health, fun, romance, shoes, etc.? I am a scuba diver and a mountain climber so sometimes I have to consider what is enough oxygen.

- List each area you would like to explore.
  - For each area, answer:
    What is too much?
    What is too little?
    What is enough?
    Go to www.TamaraGerlach.com for a PDF chart.

Gratitude:
Appreciate yourself for all that you create.

Mantra:
I am enough and I have enough.

Our Global Family

"Silently bless everyone you see or even think of today (it's impossible to do that and not start to feel happy)."

~ Marianne Williamson

We are here on this planet to connect with one another. We cannot live life alone. No matter what city, country, or socioeconomic background we come from, we are more alike than we are different. Our hearts beat together, we breathe the same air, and we radiate love and joy. In the beautiful Hawaiian language, the "ha" in Aloha means breath, and Aloha means sharing joyous breath.

The practice of kindness is one of the quickest ways to connect. When we are kind, we are embodying our radiant nature. This can mean opening a door for someone, letting him into traffic, or sharing a radiant smile that lets someone know that his inner light has been seen.

The next time you are out with a group, notice the people around you and look for the similarities. Create a connection without competition; see them, love them, and praise them for who they are. As we bless others, we are blessing ourselves as well because we are connected.

We all have our purpose, and we all work together. Some people are here to inspire us and some are here to stretch us, but they are all here to teach us. Be open to the lessons that are available from the people to whom you are connected.

It does not serve us to dwell on who is better looking, smarter, younger, or more successful. Our jealousy can spark negative thoughts that cut off the legs of others in an attempt to make ourselves feel taller. These thoughts disconnect us from our own radiant nature and from others around us.

Aligning and taking care of ourselves are crucial in order to be able to share a healthy connection with others. If we are stressed, miserable, or cut off from our Source, connecting with others in a healthy way is unlikely. We must at least take care of our basic physical, mental, and emotional needs first.

We all want to feel accepted. In earlier sections, we learned to accept ourselves, which is among our most difficult challenges, so it ought to be easier for us to accept others. Plant the seeds of compassion and appreciation in your mind.

When we realize our oneness, we can easily care for and help others because we know that, what we do to others, we do to ourselves. The opposite is also true: The care we give ourselves has an impact on others. Even if you are not ready to fully open your heart yet, you can consciously intend to do no harm to yourself or anyone else.

It doesn't stop with our connections to other humans; we share our world with plants, animals, minerals, and all forms of life. But for now, you can start by becoming aware of your connection to your human family and soak in the infinite gifts available.

Discovery Question:
Where can I let go of old beliefs and make deeper connections in my life?

Activity:
When you encounter another radiant person, notice what it is that you may feel jealous of or, reframed, what you admire about her. Then, expand your ability to be that, cultivate that in yourself, love that about her, and appreciate your new awareness.

Write down the person's name, what you see as her admirable trait (she may have many), and how you will cultivate that trait in yourself.

Gratitude:
Appreciate a person who has shown you the most about connection.

Mantra:
I gain strength from my connection to my global family.

Element II: Optimistic Attitude

"Every soul is radiant with an inner light that never dims though it may be covered over. There is no being who is not filled with beauty because each is created with a heart that is pure, a heart that beats with the rhythm of sacred life."
~ Buddha Blessings

Living with an Outrageously Optimistic Attitude

"The longer I live, the more I realize the impact of attitude on life. Attitude, to me, is more important than facts. It is more important than the past, than education, than money, than circumstances, than failures, than successes, than what other people think or say or do. It is more important than appearance, giftedness, or skill.... I am convinced that life is 10% what happens to me and 90% how I react to it. And so it is with you...we are in charge of our Attitudes."

~ Charles Swindoll

This is a beautifully written affirmation of how important attitude is to the cultivation of radiance. Attitude really is a choice and makes such a huge difference in whether we are happy or miserable. Charles Swindoll believes that life is 90% how one reacts to it. That gives us a lot of power to create our own radiant life. In the interviews I did researching this book, it became clear; universally, they reflected a theme of always having an outrageously optimistic attitude.

Living with an optimistic attitude no matter what – even when life gets difficult – will make our positive experiences even richer and make the difficult times easier to flow with. Being optimistic and surrounding ourselves with other optimistic, happy people are crucial to our radiance.

See the glass as 1/2 full.
When life gets difficult and 3/4 of your glass is gone, see it as 1/4 full.

Find the positive in everything. It is easy to see what is wrong with the world. We hear this type of scarcity thinking all of the time: I don't have enough money, I didn't get enough sleep, I don't have a job, or I don't have enough free time.

The secret is to identify what is *right* in our world: I have a pantry full of food, I have a healthy body, I have a creative mind, the sun is shining – you get the picture.

Focus on what is right, and bring your life into alignment with that. Believe that life is good and then look for evidence to prove it. Set your expectations optimistically and then aspire to fulfill them. We have already learned that what we give our energy to, we create more of. So, create an optimistic attitude about everything and then share it with others.

Discovery Question:
What is right about my life?

Activity:
Practice optimism and happiness every day:
- Be positive and cheerful.
- Be open, approachable, and friendly. Say "hi" to people on the street.
- Be honest.
- Be simple. You don't need complications and drama.
- Be generous and giving. You have plenty.
- Be kind, helpful, and supportive.
- Be enthusiastic. Life keeps getting better.

Gratitude:
Show your appreciation for all that is right in the world.

Mantra:
My optimism is unshakable.

Cultivating Playfulness

"A joy that's shared is a joy made double."

~ English proverb

There is a very playful part of cultivating radiance that includes giving ourselves full permission to have fun and live joyfully, without having to justify anything to anyone. Playfulness ignites our imaginations and our optimistic attitude. We can find fun in almost anything we do.

As a gymnastics school owner, I have trained hundreds of coaches over three decades. Part of their training focuses on how to create a lesson plan. As you can imagine, a lot goes into an hour of basic gymnastics; the new teachers have to consider the apparatus, elements, biomechanics, developmental skills and techniques, progressions, circuits, conditioning, and more. They toil over their first lesson plan until they are ready to submit it. Before even looking at it, my first question is always "What's so fun about it?" If they don't have a good answer, they're back to the drawing board. I only have to ask that question once or twice before they realize that *fun* is one of the key elements to success and must be built into everything they do.

In Marci Shimoff's book, *Happy for No Reason*, she writes of happiness as "the holy grail of human existence." It is what we all live for. Marci became so good at it that her friends started calling her the "joy bunny." How cool is that? There is a joy bunny living in all of us. Wake it up! Then start an epidemic of joy!

Connect with the pleasure and vitality of permitting yourself to get out and play! Actually plan to have fun playing every day. Turn into a 5-year-old. Let go of what anybody else thinks, and just have fun. Anyone who knocks us for having fun secretly admires our ability to be happy and wishes he had the freedom to do the same. We can inspire and give permission to others through our own freedom. Our best teachers are children; watch to see what they find amusing before they are taught to do things "right" and fear approval.

Cultivate playfulness by finding opportunities to bring forth your inner child. Children can do so many things better than adults.

For example, try skipping instead of walking. It is nearly impossible to have a bomber attitude while skipping. Here are a few things to consider (and a thousand more things can be added to the list):

- Spin until you are dizzy.
- Play games.
- Go jump in a puddle.
- Climb a tree.
- Play with a ball, hula hoop, or jump rope.
- Finger paint.
- Play tag or duck-duck-goose.
- Play on the swings and slide.
- Juggle.
- Tell jokes and riddles.
- Laugh until milk comes out your nose. Okay, maybe not.

I love having a relationship with someone who loves to play. When I want to buy Ron a gift, it's easy: he loves toys. A sweater is nice, but he'd rather have a unicycle, juggling pins, or an Indo board. (If you've never tried an Indo, check it out on the Web.) At his birthday party, among other games, he wanted stilts and a pogo stick for the guest to play with. Yes, life is never boring with this man. We also try to make sure that our closest friends are just as goofy. It keeps us physically, mentally, and spiritually fit, too!

Set yourself up for instant playfulness. My cousin, Sis Morris, keeps a small box with materials available so that if she gets the urge to scrapbook or bead, she can play without making it work.

Discovery Question:
What activities give me joy?

Activities:
- Find five ways to have fun today (and every day).
- Practice injecting fun into seemingly "un-fun" activities like meetings or sitting at your computer.

Gratitude:
Appreciate the people who show you creative ways to have fun.

Mantra:
I am radiant when I am playful!

If You See a Person Without a Smile, Give Him Yours

"Sometimes your joy is the source of your smile, but sometimes your smile can be the source of your joy."

~Thich Nhat Hanh

A simple smile or "hello!" to people as you pass by has an amazing effect on your radiance. You are *so* radiant when you smile. We light up everything and everyone around with our beauty, joy, and optimism.

Smiling actually has physiological benefits. As we stimulate different areas of our brain with positive thoughts, we smile as a "happiness reflex." Our smile releases cortisol and endorphins into our bloodstream that elevate our mood, and calm us by relaxing and softening our body.

"I have witnessed the softening of the hardest of hearts by a simple smile." ~ Goldie Hawn

We smile with our bodies. Our radiant smile begins in our heart. We start by softening our own hearts, and that energy permeates our body and comes through every cell. When our whole body is smiling, we are able to share our warmth with others. Our optimistic attitude will create plenty of spontaneous reasons to smile, but we also have the choice to smile whenever we want, for no obvious reason but to smile. :)

Don't take yourself too seriously; no one else does. Find reasons to smile and laugh often. Develop your sense of humor. Laugh at yourself when you do something silly or ridiculous. If you are not doing silly things, get to it!

Create opportunities to laugh. When others amuse you, laugh *with* them, rather than *at* them, but you don't need to laugh at hurtful or negative things. Laugh as often as possible every day. Practice finding the humor in life. If you get a little short on material, keep a few memories handy that can make you laugh in a pinch.

Discovery Question:
What inspires my radiant smile?

Activities:
- With a heartfelt, radiant smile, say "hello" to strangers. See how many will respond. This can be especially challenging in city environments, but it's really fun to watch other people light up and smile back.
- Do something goofy or daring, or anything that makes you or someone else laugh.

Gratitude:
Appreciate someone with a radiant smile.

Mantra:
My radiant smile is a gift that I am always ready to share.

Be a "Yes" Person

"It's easy to say 'no!' when there's a deeper 'yes!' burning inside."
~ Stephen R. Covey

By saying "yes" to an optimistic attitude, flexibility, and seeing the possibilities in life, we are saying a big "*yes*" to a happy life. It means accepting what life brings and keeping an open mind to what can be created from what is available. Rather than becoming attached to what we want something to be or becoming upset when life does not give us what we thought we wanted, we can be open to the possibilities and enjoy the freedom of a "yes attitude." This is illustrated beautifully in the following story: "Maybe Bad, Maybe Good."

Many years ago there was a farmer who had a horse. Horses are very valuable, so his neighbor would tell him, "What good luck you have, you have been blessed with a horse."

The farmer replied, "Maybe good, maybe bad."

One day the horse ran away and the neighbor said, "Oh, what bad luck. You lost your horse."

The farmer replied, "Maybe bad, maybe good."

The next day the horse returned with a wild mare.

The neighbor said, "What good luck. Now you have two horses".

The farmer replied, "Maybe good, maybe bad."

When the farmer's son tried to break the wild mare he was thrown and broke his leg.

The neighbor said, "Your son has a broken leg. What bad luck."

The farmer replied, "Maybe bad, maybe good."

That week soldiers came to the village to take young men to fight in a war, but the farmer's son could not go because he had a broken leg.

The neighbor said, "What luck. They will not take your son away."

The farmer replied, "Maybe good, maybe bad."

And on it goes....

When we are not attached to things or situations, but just see them as they are, we are less likely to get upset and emotionally out of alignment. This attitude is wisdom. We don't need to attach to anything because things are always changing in every moment. When you think about it, being attached or upset is totally relative.

If *my* new car gets scratched, I could become very upset. If your car gets scratched, I don't care so much. One moment we can be completely peaceful, and in the next very upset.

Seemingly "bad" experiences can turn out to be fantastic lessons. I went through a divorce a few years ago that was the best thing that ever happened to me. I just had to stay open and positive. It is okay to occasionally be dissatisfied with our lives, but we can be happy that we are aware of the imbalance and have the intelligence and resources to say "yes" to changing our situation. We never feel stuck when we realize that nothing lasts forever.

In her fantastic improv classes, Sue Walden teaches the "yes, and" game. In this game your partner comes up with an idea and your response is always "yes, and." You get to build upon their idea. Too often we hear "yes, but," which totally undermines the "yes." Try it with your family and friends, and at work. It is a fun skill to play with.

Another application of "yes, and" is to use it when setting boundaries. We can say "Yes, I will help you, and here is what I am willing to do," or "Yes, I can work late, and I am available until 6:00."

By saying "yes" to practicing an optimistic attitude, by default we are also saying "no" to the alternative of having a negative, pessimistic attitude. We say "yes" to connection with our radiant nature and a big, fun life.

Discovery Question:

What is asking to be honored in me that I really want to say "yes" to?

Activities:

- Create a "yes" list.
- Experiment with catching yourself wanting to say "no" and simply ask yourself "why?" There may be a good reason, but if it is because of fear or keeping the status quo, try a "yes" instead.

Gratitude:

Show your appreciation for people who give you the opportunity to say "yes" to your vision.

Mantra:

Yes.

"I Love It"

"I have found that if you love life, life will love you back."
~ *Arthur Rubenstein*

Building on becoming a "yes" person, we can choose to be fulfilled and content with the present. Know that it is simply what it is right now and it will change. We do have the chance, and the responsibility, to choose our attitude about it.

When we are content with what we have there is no need to be angry, complain, feel lack, or connect with some old crabby story. When we are truly content with the present moment we will always feel secure.

Even if we are not in the perfect environment or living the life of our dreams, we can use our inner joy to complete what may be lacking on the outside.

A 92-year-old, petite, poised and proud man, who is fully dressed each morning by eight o'clock, with his hair fashionably coiffed and shaved perfectly even though he is legally blind, moved to a nursing home today. His wife of 70 years recently passed away, making the move necessary. After many hours of waiting patiently in the lobby of the nursing home, he smiled sweetly when told his room was ready.

As he maneuvered his walker to the elevator, the nurse

provided a visual description of his tiny room, including the eyelet sheets that had been hung on his window.

"I love it," he stated with the enthusiasm of an 8-year-old having just been presented with a new puppy.

"Mr. Jones, you haven't seen the room; just wait."

"That doesn't have anything to do with it," he replied. "Happiness is something you decide on ahead of time. Whether I like my room or not doesn't depend on how the furniture is arranged; it's how I arrange my mind. I've already decided to love it. It's a decision I make every morning when I wake up. I have a choice: I could spend the day in bed recounting the difficulty I have with the parts of my body that no longer work or I could get out of bed and be thankful for the ones that do. Each day is a gift, and as long as my eyes open, I'll focus on the new day and all the happy memories I've stored away just for this time in my life. Old age is like a bank account. You withdraw from what you've put in. So, my advice to you would be to deposit a lot of happiness into the bank account of memories! Thank you for your part in filling my memory bank. I am still depositing."

Sweet! We can decide that we love a project at work, our new neighbor, or even airplane food (that last one is a bit more of a stretch). The point is that *we* are free to love whatever we choose to love.

Look for brilliance, radiance, and love, and you will find them.

One of the skills that Steve Zodtner, executive vice president of United States Liability Insurance, uses is to be content with what he has as he strives for excellence and success. He is a lifelong learner and uses his contagious optimism to create positive energy all around him. He loves his life and is always looking for opportunities to take it to the next level of radiance.

Being content in every moment does not mean, however, that we give up striving for more. We have been given free will and creativity. Our minds *want* to grow. We need to trust that we will know what to do when it is time without forcing life to be different than it is. So, we can "love it" *and* create more from that place.

Discovery Question:
How would my life be different if I chose to love more parts of it?

Activity:
Practice saying "I love it" at work, with your spouse, with your kids, and with the dentist. Love wherever you go and whatever you encounter. Journal your discoveries.

Gratitude:
Appreciate the people who inspire you to be even better by loving what you do.

Mantra:
I love my life!

Life Is Good and Keeps Getting Better:

Living with Gratitude and Appreciation

"When you realize your connection, you become this living, walking bundle of joy."

~ *Jolie Barretta-Keyser*

Gratitude is a feeling of thankfulness, and appreciation is our way of expressing our gratitude. When we show appreciation, we recognize the value of someone or something. Who doesn't love being appreciated?!

This was such a foundational concept in all of the interviews I did that gratitude was built into the practice of every chapter.

Make it a practice to wake up grateful every day. Express your appreciation to everyone and everything: your family, the barista, the crossing guard, the CEO, the plants, birds, airplanes, electricity, running water, sunshine, or rain. The chances of us even being born were so slim; think of all of the sperm that were wasted and the millions of things that could have gone wrong. Our very existence is a miracle.

We have good reason to appreciate what *is* working in our

lives. I have strong legs, my heart is pumping, I have a close relationship with my children, I understand myself more every day, I live with integrity, and I am kind, forgiving, and generous.

"I am a kind of paranoiac in reverse. I suspect people of plotting to make me happy." ~ J. D. Salinger

Ron and I had the good fortune of recently having had dinner with Warren Buffett. As I sat next to him, I soaked in this incredible icon. He is so passionate about life, so full of joy. He is constantly laughing and having fun. One thing that really stood out was his positive perspective on life. Okay, so he is one of the richest men on the planet, and that kind of wealth could make you pretty happy, but his joy came from an organic place. He really believes that life will just keep getting better. He pointed out that as a country, we have only been around a little over 230 years, and look at the progress we have made. We are a nation of innovative creators, and he doesn't see that changing anytime soon. If we truly look at the improvements that have been made even within our own lifetimes, it is inspiring.

He shared a story that he uses to teach young people when they start thinking they have it hard:

Imagine a barrel with six billion tickets in it; one for each person on earth. You can put your ticket back in and pull out 100 others and choose which one you'd like to trade places with. Fifty percent of those 100 will be of the opposite gender from yours. Eighty percent would be impoverished.

To expand on that, 70% would be illiterate, 6% would have 59% of the wealth, and all of those would be American. Fifty percent would be hungry or suffer from malnutrition, 1% will be dying, and 1% have just been born.

Puts things into perspective, doesn't it? I wouldn't choose to put my ticket back in. If you are reading this book, you are in the 30% of the world's population that can read, and the 20% that have enough money to buy a book. We have already won the lottery of life; let's live with more gratitude and appreciation.

Discovery Question:
What am I grateful for in my life?

Activity:
Write down five things that you are grateful for every day for one week (or longer). You can go to gratitudelog.com for inspiration and to create your own on-line list.

Gratitude:
Who has taught you the most about gratitude and appreciation?

Mantra:
I cultivate acceptance and gratitude no matter what the situation.

Using Obstacles as a Springboard

"The only real prison is fear, and the only real freedom is freedom from fear."

~ Aung San Suu Kyi

We all face obstacles in our lives. The difference is that when we are being radiant, obstacles don't stop us. Obstacles are merely resistance from the outside that can be used to our advantage. Resistance can be a good thing, like when we are walking on ice; we need some resistance to get to where we are going.

When we dis-empower ourselves and act the victim, perceived obstacles look more like pits than springboards.

Rather than think, "Oh, man. I *have* to deal with this," we can have the attitude of "Yes! I *get* to deal with this." Some of us are chosen to overcome some really difficult obstacles in our lives, *and* we are given the tools to create from them in order to inspire, teach, and give hope to others.

My mother was a great gymnastics teacher. She used to give her students strengthening drills as a reward for doing well. All the other teachers wondered why her athletes were always so happy to do push-ups, pull-ups, sit-ups, etc. They were not told they "had to," but believed that they "got to" do their drills. She told them it was a reward of an even stronger body. How many of us have done a workout because we felt we "had to"? Let's practice a more positive perspective.

Obstacles can be physical: a 24-hour clock or distractions like the computer, TV, phone, work, laundry, or (insert your personal obstacle here). Those obstacles can be easier to manage. The sneaky obstacles are more often found in our mind. Here are a few obstacles many of us experience, and how we can choose to respond to them.

Fear

Underlying almost any obstacle is fear. Oftentimes, behind our biggest fear lies our biggest passion – something that our spirit must do. It's when we are most passionate about something and want to do it well that the fear of failure or rejection may be present. Our fears will undermine, sabotage, and kill our dreams. It gets in the way of compassion for others and ourselves. We must have the courage to feel fear but not let it stop us.

As part of becoming a man, the Achuar Indians of the Amazon send young men into the rainforest for days on psychoactive herbs to discover themselves and uncover their biggest fears through visions. While visiting the rainforest, Ron and I met Octavio, who took us to the waterfall where he had his vision and shared the story of his quest. The vision representing his fear was a huge, angry panther. At the time, he did not know whether it was real or not. He did know that he had to face his fear to become a man. So, he went toward the growling panther, reached out, and touched it. At that moment he embodied the power of the animal. His fear became his strength, and it shows through his radiance.

Limiting Beliefs

Not doing enough, or being enough, or perfectionism – these are a total buzz-kill. Trying to be perfect sucks the joy out of anything we do because, no matter how much we do, or how well we do it, we'll never be good enough. It is hard to get motivated to do a project when we have already made up that it won't be good enough.

When we criticize ourselves, we give others permission to criticize us. No matter how badly we beat ourselves up, it feels even worse coming from someone else, and adds evidence to our limiting beliefs.

Our job is to do the best we can without comparing ourselves or being in competition with anyone, just being human, real, and the best we can be in every moment and always growing and moving past limiting beliefs.

Delusions

This is not seeing or not wanting to even consider the reality of what is happening in our life – sticking our head in the sand or other dark places. Being delusional definitely does not make us radiant. It puts us into a cycle of repeating the same mistakes because we do not want to see reality. By becoming aware of our delusions, they are no longer obstacles; they are now lessons from which we can change and grow.

Guilt

Doing anything out of guilt, because we "should," or feeling selfish for taking care of ourselves gets in the way of our radiance. When we give ourselves permission to be authentic and do the things that move us toward harmony, freedom, and radiance, it is easier to let go of feelings of guilt.

Once in a Sunday evening restorative yoga class the teacher asked who felt guilty about being there. I was the *only* woman who did not raise my hand. It clearly demonstrated how prevalent our feelings of guilt are. And those are only the women who showed up! How many others passed on the opportunity to restore their body and mind because they felt guilty about it?

As we shift our beliefs from the guilt of feeling undeserving or unworthy, we make a connection with what gives us joy. Don't let guilt rip off your radiance.

Obligation

We *do* have obligations to others, but we can take it too far by giving what we don't have. We say things like "my kids/spouse/parents/work/friends need me." Yes! True! Be healthier *for* them. We cannot let our obligations exhaust us. We can balance our time with energy giving obligations and the ability to say "no." Our first obligation is to take care of ourselves.

Sometimes we feel obligated because we don't want to hurt someone else.

> There once was a woman who would visit Father Tom every Sunday after church to complain about her husband. "He is so lazy...he is so arrogant... he drinks too much". She would go on and on like this for several weeks.
>
> One day Father Tom finally said to her, "You are obviously very unhappy. I have to ask, why did you marry him?"
>
> She said, "Well, I had to."
>
> When Father Tom asked why, she replied, "Because he asked me."

When I heard this story, I laughed and laughed, until it suddenly occurred to me that I had been engaged *five* times and married twice – because someone asked! I felt obligated and couldn't say no. I'm over that now. Go ahead – ask me to marry you.

Hiding or Holding Back

This shows up when we don't fully commit to what we are capable of and don't fully bloom. We hesitate when we feel like there is a chance of failing or looking stupid. We hide when we are afraid of being disappointed or disappointing others. Our self-critic says things like "Don't do it," "You'll screw it up," or "It doesn't matter," when really our heart's desire is to grow. Realize that hiding and holding back gets us the exact opposite of what we actually want.

None of us wake up and say, "I think I'd like to make my life complicated and difficult today." We all want to simplify our lives and be our best. By becoming aware of our obstacles, we can create new outcomes in our life.

Not only live with, but embrace your obstacles. Love them as the greatest teachers in your life. Don't let your fears sabotage you, but use them to motivate you and take you to the next level. Let's turn fear into confidence, delusions into awareness, hiding into growth and connection, and obligation into self-care. You will find obstacles everywhere, and therefore more opportunities to cultivate your radiance.

Discovery Questions:
What do I want to activate in my life?
>Examples: love, acceptance, connection, harmony, abundance, health, serenity, connection to Source.

Why?

Activities:
- Write down what is stopping you from having what you want in your life right now and what triggers those obstacles.
- Write down how you will recover from being triggered and shift the obstacle into a springboard.

Gratitude:
Appreciate the times you have made it through difficult obstacles, what you learned, and how it felt to be on the other side.

Mantra:
I have the courage to do anything.

Well, Excuse Me

"Ninety-nine percent of the failures come from people who have the habit of making excuses."

~ *George Washington Carver*

Excuses are one of our biggest obstacles and also a real energy drain. Excuses are not reasons. They are just excuses. When we are not being completely honest with others and ourselves, or are not living in alignment with what we really want, excuses show up. We limit ourselves by making excuses for why we did something or can't do something.

Becoming aware of our excuses is the first step. Then we can give ourselves an "excusectomy." Cut out the blockage and be honest with ourselves. Put our big pants on and be responsible. Instead of complicating things with words that keep us from radiance, we can clarify our thoughts and align our actions to take us where we want to go in our relationships and our lives.

My partner, Ron, taught me a great lesson about being responsible instead of making an excuse. When he is late, rather than telling people about how bad traffic was, how a phone call took too long, or giving some other lame excuse, he simply says, "I am sorry that I am late. I did not allow enough time to get here". People are often shocked because they are *expecting* an excuse. Ron speaks the truth and takes responsibility. It's like a breath of fresh air, and nobody's intelligence gets insulted. He's an incredibly radiant man, my obvious bias aside.

Let's designate excuse-free zones, starting in our own head.

When we make excuses about why we cannot accomplish something, we are giving away our power. We choose to become a victim of something seemingly outside of our control when in reality, most of what we make excuses for *is* within our control when we change our beliefs and attitude, and live with passion and vision.

There are entire websites dedicated to helping people come up with excuses, and, having worked with thousands of athletes and coaches over the years, I have heard some doozies.

I encourage you to read Shel Silverstein's poem "Sick." In the poem a child goes through a hilarious litany of excuses about why she is too sick to go to school. At the end she says, "What's that you say? You say today is...Saturday? G'bye, I'm going out to play!"

Funny how we can put so much effort into getting out of what we don't enjoy and be ready to go for something we love. It may be time to take an honest look at what we are making excuses about and deciding if we can change our attitude, or if it belongs on our "drains" list.

Discovery Question:
What excuses limit me?

Activity:
For *one* day do not make one single excuse – not even to yourself. Take responsibility for everything. It can be more difficult than it sounds until we practice it. If it feels good, continue to do it every day.

Gratitude:
Appreciate people who take responsibility rather than make excuses.

Mantra:
My integrity and responsibility turn up my radiance.

Delight in Change

"It is not the strongest of the species that survives, nor the most intelligent, but the one most responsive to change."

~ Charles Darwin

As we become more connected to our radiance, we see that change is a wonderful part of the process. Two of the most limiting phrases in any language are "I can't change" and "I don't like change."

Everything we experience is in a state of change. It is what keeps us alive. If we weren't constantly exchanging the air in our lungs or the blood in our heart, we would keel over. Clearly, we *are* good at change; we do it all the time. It only becomes challenging when we are attached to the way things were or how we wanted them to be.

Let's choose to love change, to delight in it, and to see it as opportunity for growth. We can welcome change with an optimistic attitude by appreciating that something really positive will come from it. Sometimes we just have to open our eyes and stop resisting in order to see the great stuff that can come from change.

"If we don't change soon, we'll end up where we are going." ~ Irwin Corey

---

Some dramatic changes happen quickly, like winning the lottery, or receiving an unexpected pink slip or "Dear John" letter. We may be suddenly thrown into changes that we may not be ready for. Other changes happen more slowly, like training to be a doctor or an Olympian, or learning to parent. We may experience sudden realizations that change us instantly. For example, when we become connected to our radiant nature, we are changed in that moment. As soon as we feel ourselves flipping out and our resistance to change arising, we can choose a new attitude – one of grace.

Life is about change. Things change, people change, thoughts change: heck, I even changed my underwear this morning. Getting stuck in wanting things not to change will only cause us to suffer.

Being a role model for change inspires others. Be compassionate with yourself and others as you begin to change. Remember that in the stages of cultivation, we may fall many times, learn, make adjustments, and then learn some more, before we can flow through change smoothly.

Discovery Question:
How will changing my attitude create freedom in my life?

Activity:
Write down the changes have you resisted in each area of your life:
- Physical body,
- Relationships,
- Physical environment,
- Career,
- Financial, and
- Growth.

Next, choose how you will delight in changing each of these things and the radiance that will be cultivated.
Then do it.

Gratitude:
Appreciate yourself for being open and accepting change.

Mantra:
My ability to change keeps me in the flow and moving forward.

21

Practicing Infinite Patience

"Our patience will achieve more than our force."

~ Edmund Burke

Infinite patience. This means that our patience has no end. I know it's difficult to imagine, but it can be practiced every day.

A young monk was living in the mountains in a small hut with only a flap of fabric for a door. One day he went inside to meditate. He sat, prepared his body, and began to meditate. Just then, a cat came in and sat on his lap. He calmly picked up the cat and took it outside. He returned to meditating. The cat came back in and climbed back onto the monk's lap. He got up and took the cat out again. This dance went on for quite some time when the monk finally yelled at the cat, "Stay out! Can't you see that I am trying to meditate?!" Then he realized that he had allowed the cat to completely disturb his serenity. With this realization, he went back in and sat. The cat came back in and climbed up on his lap, only this time the monk did not react: He just continued to meditate with a peaceful mind. After thirty seconds or so, the cat got up and left.

Ironically, the monk's patience created the result he wanted. We can practice by taking our time with whatever we do and allowing others to do the same. There is an element of trust that comes with a patient attitude. We trust that what needs to happen will exactly when it is supposed to, all in time. It takes a belief that there is a bigger plan than ours.

When we want to grow a tree, we don't pull on the sprout to make it grow faster; we wait. It also would make no sense to irrigate the branches; we irrigate the roots. We don't water it all at once; we water it every day until it has established deep roots and will grow on its own.

Impatience is often the cause of our imbalance, disconnection, and those words and actions that we wish we could take back. It serves us to take a second to stop thinking that what we want is so dang important and let our false ego take a backseat. Then, smile and be graceful.

When it comes to our life dreams, practicing patience can be the most difficult. The beauty of it is in the fact that we must be patient is what makes them our life dreams. If we had developed ourselves and learned all of the lessons we needed, we would already have accomplished them. When we hold our vision patiently, it will happen in time.

The practice of patience is an empowering experience. Our ability to respond rather than react is true freedom and enhances our radiance. All we need to do is take a deep breath, get centered, and chill out.

Discovery Question:
What am I allowing to disturb my serenity?

Activities:
- Be deliberate with your actions. Practice eating patiently, talking and listening patiently, moving with intention and ease, and being in the moment of what you are doing without forcing it to be over.
- We so often hear that we should "be in the moment." Let's actually practice it. Try patience in traffic, at the store, with a

coworker, or with a child tying her shoes. Find opportunities to practice infinite patience every day.

Gratitude:
Appreciate the people who have been patient with you, and pass it on.

Mantra:
I practice infinite patience.

Element III: Passion

"There is one quality which one must possess to win, and that is definiteness of purpose, the knowledge of what one wants, and a burning desire to possess it." ~Napoleon Hill

Cultivating Passion:

Passion in Action

"We did not come here to be common.... We did not travel this great distance to give up, give in and lie down. We came here to wake up and be joyful; to stand up and be powerful; to open up our hearts, our minds and our eyes as we expand our knowledge and our perception. You are extraordinary and you are powerful beyond belief!"

~ Heather K. O'Hara

Giving attention to our passion wakes up every cell in our body. We tingle, our heart races, and we feel completely alive. Our job is to find what we are interested in and be willing to let go of thinking that we know everything.

Discover life through the eyes of a child; be passionate about the adventure – not knowing, accepting, and cultivating our passion. When we think we already have all of the answers, we diminish radiance. On the other hand, being open and willing creates it. Reach out for new ways of seeing the world.

Cultivating passion is a constant evolution. Passion for something specific can change over time. Sometimes we're hot, sometimes we're not. We haven't lost our passion altogether; we may have just lost it for that specific thing. That just means it's time to cultivate our passion for something new that we will grow into, something that makes us want to jump out of bed in the morning.

If you want to have a passionate, creative, and radiant life, you must wake up every day and practice being passionate, creative, and radiant!

We can find creative ways to do our "regular" life: new ways to communicate, work, grow, and stretch our comfort zone. Dare to be brilliant!

As part of the interviews for this book, I posed the question: "What are you passionate about?" Some people had specific things that they were super passionate about, but the standard answer was "life." Radiant people know that passion is essential.

Patrick J. Ryan, author of *Awakened Wisdom: A Guide to Reclaiming Your Brilliance*, had an experience where he died and was brought back to life. This is not figurative; he literally died and was resuscitated. After having that experience, he realized that death wasn't so bad; there was no need to fear it, so he went about living his life fully with great passion and purpose. Among his specific passions is racecar driving.

Some people get their wake-up call in the form of cancer or a heart attack. Let's not wait for such a wake-up call; let's get passionate about life now.

Being passionate about life is living life to its fullest, to the edge, doing the absolute best we can, not being content with a boring, tedious, mundane life. Walk boldly into life; don't slink in. We become what we practice. If you are not passionate about your life, trust me, no one else is going to be.

Embrace life with a full heart, spark your creativity, inspire, give your life meaning, rediscover what you love, or discover new passions, but please, please, please cultivate your passion.

Discovery Question:
What makes me come alive?

Activities:
- Make passion a priority.
- Make your challenge trying to decide *which* passion to follow today.
- Leave no doubt in anyone's mind, especially your own, that you are a passionate person.
- Don't be satisfied with surface passion. Go deep, and keep asking yourself "why" you are passionate. More joy will be revealed.

Gratitude:
Appreciate your own passions and the people in your life who model passion.

Mantra:
I am passionate about my life!

23

Dream Big!

"DARE to believe in your dreams – you would never have been given the dream in the first place and have the seed placed in your heart without being given the tools and the means to achieve it."
~Francine Allaire

Francine Allaire had a soul dream to create the Daring Woman Network, where she encourages women to reclaim their life and live by design, not default. She is passion in action and a great role model because she completely lives her life embodying that passion. She told me that she loves her life so much that she wishes she didn't have to sleep, and being outside of her comfort zone is her way of life. She is always on the edge of excitement and fear, and it shows, because this woman sizzles.

Our dreams are what we live for. They are our mind's glimpse into the future we are creating. Having a radiant life begins with a dream.

Our dreams give us direction. Our dreams are so *big* that they cannot be quantified, but are ever expanding. They cannot be captured and put into a box, nor written down and kept neatly in a binder on our shelf. Big dreams are filled with enthusiasm, and sometimes they feel risky, messy, and uninhibited.

Big dreams not only inspire us, but everyone around us.

There is little in this world that is more impressive than a person living her dream.

Walt Disney, one of our most famous dreamers, told us that if we'd only "wish upon a star," our dreams would come true. He was a role model for success and admitted that it takes more than just wishing; we must have passion, vision, planning, and hard work to make our dreams come true.

There is no need to let "reality" get in the way of your dreams. Big dreamers change the world. Not long ago many would have said that people can't fly, visit the moon, or breathe underwater, but somebody dreamed they could. Don't hang out with people who tell you to "get real."

We all face challenges to dreaming big. We have to work, pay the bills, care for others – and the list of "musts" goes on. We really have to look at what is at stake if we stop dreaming big. We may be ripping off ourselves and the rest of the world from experiencing our radiance.

Big dreams don't die with us. The difference between goals and dreams is that goals are quantifiable: "I want to own my own business." This is easily quantified because you either own it or you don't, and when you die, you won't. To get to the dream, we have to ask ourselves "why." "I want to create a business where people discover themselves". That lives beyond us. That is where the magic is.

If you do what you love, you will be more fulfilled; believe that you already have what you need to live it. Be outrageous, be creative, and dream big.

Discovery Questions:
What do I want most out of life?
How are my dreams an agent for change?

Activity:
Create a "dream list." Write down those things that you have always wanted to do, but have put on the back burner. It is fine if they are goals, too.

Then ask why you want to do each.

Look for common threads and develop your big dream.

Have the courage to share your dream with the world.

Get started today!

Gratitude:

Be grateful for your dreams of the past that have made you successful and your ability to build on them.

Mantra:

Dreams come true.

Radiant Inspiration Is Everywhere

"There never was a great soul that did not have some divine inspiration."

~ *Marcus Tullius Cicero*

When we are inspired we feel totally alive. We are connected and imaginative, and ready to discover possibilities and create.

If we just look around we can find inspiration for our radiance everywhere: in art, design, nature, reading, people watching, animals, or music. We can be inspired by everything. Look for what embodies radiance.

We can also find inspiration in ourselves by slowing down and asking our heart, mind, and body what wants to be expressed. In Patrick J. Ryan's *Awakened Wisdom: Guide to Reclaiming Your Brilliance* book and program, he teaches us to check in with our wisdom fields to keep us on track and moving forward.

When we are centered we become conduits for inspiration to move through. We may suddenly notice creative ideas emerging, ready to be born into action, or inspiration might come slowly like the unfolding of the petals of the flower of our mind. We begin to see one thing, and then another, and then another.

Being inspired is not some form of magic, nor a secret that we must learn. It is simply about believing in ourselves and, mostly, not stopping ourselves from acting on our inspirations. Think of all that we would be missing if the great artists, chefs, inventors, and leaders of the world shut down their inspiration.

As a choreographer, I find inspiration in the branches of a tree, the way wax melts, or what happens inside my body when I hear music or am moved by a story. If I look and listen for inspiration, movement just comes through me. It is certainly not about being safe and comfortable; it is alive and exciting. It is about giving myself permission to do what I love with passion.

While writing this book, I let inspiration move through me, and I just typed. It didn't have to make sense or be beautiful at the time, but there were times that words, like dance, moved through me. Of course there is always lots of room to "fine-tune" our creation, as long as we don't fine-tune it to death.

Blend inspiration from several sources to create a radiance that is unique to you.

All great creators have had muses. Find yours. Be where you are and look at what is possible from there. I mean literally – from where you physically are right now, take a moment to look around and notice what moves your soul: a picture, the shape of a chair, the sunlight, or the sound of wind chimes.

Just notice and let inspiration be stirred in you.

Discovery Question:
What inspires my radiance?

Activities:
- Find inspiration in ten (or 100) different ways throughout your day.
- Let inspiration move you. Follow it without trying to control it. Let it light you up.

Gratitude:
Appreciate the greatest inspirational people and things in your life.

Mantra:
I find inspiration in everyone and everything.

NGU

(Never Give Up)

"The harder you work, the harder it is to surrender."
~ Vince Lombardi

It takes courage and diligence to live a passionate, radiant life. By always doing our best and having the right motivation, we can go beyond our perceived limitations. The right motivation comes from our intentions to serve the highest purpose rather than our false ego, so we are willing to risk failure and make mistakes in service of excellence.

The NGU attitude is so important to cultivating radiance because we are learning many new skills and creating new habits. Our diligence and discipline will pay off as we reach for our very worthy dream of living with positive beliefs, an optimistic attitude, passion, alignment, and vision.

The good news is that *we* are 100% responsible for the level of passion in our life. It completely comes from inside of us. Choosing to give up on our passion is a form of self-abuse. Don't give up on yourself before anyone else has a chance to. It is foundational to our self-respect.

Long ago, Mike Lynch, Olympic Gold Medal Coach, had a goal of owning an Indian motorcycle. They run about $50K, which he did not have at the time. He decided that he would start buying original Indian parts, and little by little he built his own bike for $6K.

He did not let the fact that he originally didn't have the money stop him, and he never gave up on his passion-driven goal. He is now an expert on restoring Indian motorcycles and has worked with collectors all over the world.

Although creating and beginning to practice our radiance plan will have some immediate benefits, many more benefits will come as we continue to cultivate our radiance. When we least expect it, amazing shifts will occur.

"When you feel in your gut what you are and then dynamically pursue it – don't back down and don't give up – then you're going to mystify a lot of folks."

~ Bob Dylan

A radiant young gymnast named Tiffany trained with me since she was about 4 years old. At age 7 she began to go to competitions with the team. She was always very talented and at the top of her divisions for years, but not a "rock star." When she was about 11, I took her to a National Junior Olympic competition. The other coaches came up to me and asked, "Where did you get this girl? She is beautiful!" as if she had dropped out of the sky. I told them it was Tiffany, the same girl that they have been seeing for years. In their eyes, she had "suddenly" become talented. The reality was that she had trained for two-thirds of her life, rarely missing a practice and *always* giving her best with a positive attitude at practices and competitions. That is what it takes to be an "overnight success." Tiffany is now a touring professional dancer, and living a passionate, courageous, and diligent life because she has an NGU attitude.

The best time to practice NGU is when life is most challenging or difficult. When we feel like giving up or chickening out, we can choose to refresh our attitude and reconnect with our passion. It is like when our computer starts acting crazy: We turn it off, wait a few moments, and reboot. We can do the same thing, and start our day over or change our pattern of thinking at any moment.

Never give up on the things you love in order to do things that don't matter.

We can ask ourselves for a do-over. When we realize we are doing something that goes against our radiance plan or makes us feel icky, ask for a do-over. If something is not working for us, we can change it as soon as we are aware. We don't have to be stuck with our old way of doing things, especially if we want to be radiant.

Discovery Question:
What does NGU mean in my life?

Activity:
Using the things from your dream big list, write down how you will light your own fire when it gets difficult.

Gratitude:
Appreciate someone who shows the NGU spirit.

Mantra:
NGU!

The Passion of Adventure

"I am not an adventurer by choice but by fate."

~ *Vincent van Gogh*

*A*lways love what you do and love your life – because you create it. Each day we can make an intention to passionately shake our world into greatness through creativity, innovation, and adventure.

Once we get started living with this level of passion and courage, we take on a whole new level of radiance. We can't help but bring joy, light, and optimism into our life with this approach. It is impossible to create from our connection to Source, to gather inspiration from all that is around us, to co-create with the Universe, and to be pessimistic at the same time. Our Source wants us to inspire each other and gives us all that we need to do so. When our spirit is strong, there is less fear in risk.

I bought my first business, Encore Gymnastics, in 1989, and I joke about having the fear that one day a client would walk into my office, point at me, and say, "You don't know what you are doing!" and I would drop my head onto my desk and say, "You're right." It was a very realistic fear, because I really *don't* know what I am doing. That's good! My staff and I are creating things that have not been done before in our market. We've never let the fact that something hasn't been done before stop us. Fortunately, most of our ideas have gone well and the business thrives.

Virginia Kelley, Encore's business director, says, "We teach our students that risk is good. They train hard, and sometimes doing a skill for the first time is scary, but if they are prepared properly, they are successful and gain confidence. If we are teaching our students to live with courage, we'd better be doing it ourselves." It is an exciting adventure for all of us to create something magnificent from that daring place – from that place of not knowing how it will turn out, while willing to take a chance.

"You need chaos in your soul to give birth to a dancing star." ~Nietzsche

We are born to be adventurous. That is why it is so much fun to explore. We can swing out beyond the edges of our comfort zone – at times, way beyond – and sometimes we go flying off, but we always land in something better. We don't always get what we thought we would, but we always get something new and gain experience.

When we are tapped into our wisdom, we can explore the possibilities by taking risks with wisdom. This is not risk for the sake of risk, but in order to serve a higher purpose, support our dream, and fulfill our purpose.

If you're not afraid sometimes, you are probably living a boring, beige life. Start living in colors bold and bright. Sometimes the most adventurous thing is to just get started on passionately living our dreams.

Discovery Questions:
What is asking to be born in me?
What would I do if I knew I could not fail?

Activity:
Practice taking "risks with wisdom":

- Write down some of the possibilities that are available to you, but that you have been afraid to risk.
- Get honest with yourself and look at what is really stopping you. Be aware of deluded or self-critical thoughts.
- Ask youself: What is a possible next step?
- Commit to taking action. This can look like adventure, or it could be letting something go, remembering the "wisdom" part.

Gratitude:
Appreciate the people who have taught you the most about living a passionate, adventurous life.

Mantra:
I am an adventurous spirit.

Living with an Open Heart

"You give but little when you give of your possessions. It is when you give of yourself that you truly give."

~Kahlil Gibran

Opening our heart can be one of the most adventurous things we'll ever do. I know people who'd be willing to bungee jump before they'd be willing to open their heart. Vulnerability can be scary, but it is vital to our radiance. If we are not loving and risking with our whole heart, we are not fully alive.

This is where many deluded thoughts can appear. We might hear that voice in our head saying things like "Remember what happened last time?" "If you show them your heart, they will reject you," "You might get hurt; better hold back," and our self-critic's favorite, "If they really knew me, they wouldn't like me; I am not a good person."

Again, this is when we get to observe that voice and thank it for attempting to keep the status quo, but instead we do what our radiant heart wants. It is about saying "Yes. I am willing to live authentically, boldly, with an open heart and no attachment to the opinion of others."

I have the honor of being the life coach to a bright and beautiful woman whose heart had been continually broken in unspeakable ways by the people she loved since her childhood. She had all but shut down to love. After several months of working together, she felt strong, confident, and ready to be vulnerable and to open her heart. She began a new romantic relationship and, although it was very difficult at first to change her habits and truly open her heart, with her newly acquired tools, this time she was able to lovingly step into the adventure and is enjoying the deepest relationship of her life. She had to open her heart to herself and believe that she was worthy of love before love could come flooding in.

First we must open our hearts to connect with our Source of radiance. Then we can open it to others. We connect with our heart by giving it attention and listening to what it needs. As soon as we shift our attention, we will start giving our heart what it needs. We can't force our heart open, but we can encourage it to blossom.

What you nurture will blossom.
Cultivate your passions, strengths, and ability to flourish, and then share the fruits.

Life will test our willingness to stay open. It is easy to be open with people who you already like or love, but what about those who make it difficult?

Recently, I was at the grocery store smiling at everybody like I do. One man looked back at me like a wolf looking at a lamb. Now, I may be vulnerable, but one thing I am not is weak. He had clearly misinterpreted my friendliness. I could have labeled him as a creep and shut down. Instead, I chose to have compassion for his confusion and connect with his radiant nature – to see him for what is in his heart. Of course, this was a very public situation and I felt safe. When he passed by me a second time, his energy had completely changed; he was radiant. Not a word was exchanged, but a heart connection had been made.

In India and Nepal they greet each other with the Sanskrit word *Namaste,* meaning "I bow (reverently) to you" but often translated as "my higher self recognizes your higher self." In Zulu the greeting translates to "I see you," with the response of "I am here." These are two beautiful examples of how a simple greeting can inspire opening our heart, being present, and connecting with others.

There may be people with whom we have difficulty connecting, and that is okay. Keep looking for their radiance; it is in there somewhere. We can always remain open for healthy, loving connection. It's like saying "my heart is open, take all that you need, I have plenty, and there will always be more."

Discovery Question:
What does it mean to live with an open heart?

Activities:
- Practice keeping your heart open and available from a strong, centered place of deep connection to your own radiance.
- Visualize your heart energy radiating from you and waking sleeping hearts.
- Practice acknowledging people with reverence.

Gratitude:
Appreciate your ability to risk being vulnerable and live with an open heart.

Mantra:
My most daring adventure is to live with an open heart.

The Passion of Our Life Purpose

"More people fail because of lack of purpose than do because of a lack of talent."

~ *Billy Sunday*

We all want to be well used. No matter what challenges we have had in our lives, we want to reach our potential and live our lives to the fullest. We know we are living from the passion of our life purpose when it wakes up our soul, it comes easily and naturally to us, and, like our radiance super-powers, we are able to do it without self-criticism.

If we look at why we are here, on this planet, at this time, there are some universal parallels. We are all called to connect with others, to express ourselves, to have an impact or make a difference, to love and be loved, and to learn. Assume that all of these things are true for you as well. Each of us then gets to add in our own special spice: our purpose.

We all lived with the passion of our purpose easily as children. Some of us developed it; some of us forgot. Clarifying it can be really easy if we don't try to intellectualize it too much. We are all given strengths and talents to support our purpose. Our soul knows what makes us come alive and calls us to do it.

Honor the wisdom of your purpose. Think of your life purpose as the job you were put on earth to do. We are all a piece of the big puzzle, and our job is to find the space we are meant to fill.

"When you do something you love with passion and perseverance, you are already a success."

~ *Jack Canfield*

Our passions are an indicator of our purpose. We must *love* our purpose; it must be the most exciting thing in our life – the thing we cannot live without, and something that comes easily and naturally to us. Every deeply fulfilling thing that we do is motivated by our purpose.

The passion of living our life purpose is in serving someone or something in such a way that we are totally enthusiastic and devoted. It is a childlike giddiness that invites us to play to the fullest.

My life purpose is to create freedom, and I have done this throughout my life. I create freedom for others and myself. Whether it is through teaching children how to use their bodies in gymnastics or guiding my coaching clients out of feeling stuck, this is what I do. In my life it has shown up as the ability to simultaneously own several different businesses, travel all over the world, spend time with friends and family, practice arts and sports, volunteer, and have time to write books. My life purpose is *why* I am writing books.

When we discover our life purpose, it is an incredibly liberating feeling. We give ourselves permission to do everything with that in our heart. We do things that we never imagined were possible. Even the simplest tasks will be brought to greatness.

Our life purpose is not our career, but oftentimes we have chosen careers that fulfill our purpose.

"Think enthusiastically about everything; but especially about your job. If you do, you'll put a touch of glory in your life. If you love your job with enthusiasm, you'll shake it to pieces. You'll love it into greatness." ~Norman Vincent Peale

Doug is a checker at our local grocery store. I don't know whether he has defined his purpose, but it is working for him and manifests through his radiance. He brings such joy to his customers and makes each one feel so special. He greets people as they walk into the store, usually by name, and is genuinely happy to see us.

"Daily ripples of excellence-overtime-become a tsunami of success." ~ Robin Sharma

In Robin Sharma's book *The Leader Who Had No Title*, he beautifully illustrates how we can bring passion, purpose, and greatness into everything we do. Even the simplest tasks can be done with purpose and not only affect our own fulfillment, but have a positive impact on everyone we touch.

When we are conscious of our purpose, we mindfully create from it. As you create your personal Radiance Plan, be sure that it aligns with your purpose. Include your life purpose in your daily self-care. Give yourself opportunities to live with purpose every day. When you live from your purpose you can't go wrong.

We know when we are living our purpose because we are not living someone else's idea of who we should be.

If you are not sure of your life purpose, it's okay. At least get curious, start to explore, or guess for now; it will be revealed to you in time. You can also ask for help from a professional coach who specializes in life purpose work.

Discovery Questions:
What is my life purpose?
What must my life include to fulfill my purpose?

Activity:
Sit quietly for a few minutes focusing on your breathing, and then ask yourself these questions:

- What am I passionate about? (This can include many things.)
- Why does it make me feel so alive?
- What common themes or strengths have been dominant throughout my life? (You may want to look back at old journal entries. When did you feel most alive?)
- What is present when I feel successful or radiant?
- What do I do easily and without self-criticism?
- What would be my "dream job"? (Be creative and don't let reality or finances get in your way. It could be teaching children in Peru, or building hang gliders. You don't have to actually quit your job to go do it, but it will give you clues on your purpose.)

Now look for the underlying *action* that supports the answers to these questions. Remember: Our life purpose is what we are here to *do*.

To help you get a feel, a few of my client's life purposes include to:

- Empower
- Paint with words
- Guide
- Discover
- Create beauty
- Hold accountable
- Engage
- Create light
- Explore
- Design

They do each of these things in their own unique way.

Gratitude:
Appreciate a role model that is living the passion of their life purpose.

Mantra:
I live from my purpose with ease and passion.

Element IV:
Self-Care
Alignment

By making investments in our physical, mental, and spiritual alignment, we will never go bankrupt.

Foundation for Radiant Alignment

"For beautiful eyes, look for the good in others; For beautiful lips, speak only words of kindness; and for poise, walk with the knowledge that you are never alone."

~ Audrey Hepburn

Can you relate to the pattern of running on high – go, go, go – until you hit the wall? We get stressed, exhausted, and out of alignment. Then, we do just enough self-care to jump back in, full-speed ahead. Crash, rinse, repeat.

It's okay if we want to live at full-speed, but first we must create a foundation that can support that pace. Think of what you would be capable of if you just took a few minutes each day to recharge, center, and breathe.

Radiant people exercise their optimism, empowerment, and passions through self-care. Treat self-care like a muscle that needs training, or a skill that is done so many times that radiance becomes engrained into daily life as an easy, natural part of our being. We change the game by choosing to create a strong foundation of self-care and radiance.

Stacking Our Bricks Right

Alignment is vital to a foundation. Can you imagine building a wall of brick where you put bricks down randomly and were sporadic about using mortar? In the end, the wall you'd have built would be weak – a disaster waiting to happen.

The random approach to self-care creates imbalance and dims our light.

You will know you are out of alignment when:

- You are looking to others for validation, nurturing, or answers,
- You are stressed, overwhelmed, or drained,
- You are complaining, cranky, or have a bomber attitude, and
- You have lost the joy, playfulness, and appreciation from your life.

To quote David Byrne of the Talking Heads, "How did I get here?" There are points in our lives when we slow down long enough to look around and wonder how it all happened.

Working ourselves into exhaustion may have become such a familiar feeling that it feels "normal" and we don't even realize how tired we have become.

A good way to discover what is running you to exhaustion is to ask yourself these questions:

When we feel out of alignment, HALT and ask if we are:
Hungry
Angry
Lonely
Tired

- What have I eaten today/ this week?
- How nutritious were my meals?
- What do I need to let go of? Am I holding on to a resentment or negative attitude?
- What am I putting into my head? Is it positive news, readings, and music?

- Who am I hanging out with? Are they faucets or drains?
- Am I connected to Source and others?
- How many continuous hours of sleep did I get last night or on average this week?
- How much time have I taken to recharge my battery today/ this week? Count each workout, walk, meditation, or whatever you do to recharge.
- Am I doing everything for everyone, except me?

You will know when you are *in* alignment when:
- You are taking care of yourself physically, mentally, and spiritually,
- You light up and have plenty of creative energy,
- Your radiance is rubbing off on the people around you,
- You are patient and compassionate, and
- You express your appreciation for all of the good in your life.

Awareness of Alignment

Since alignment is an ever-changing state, we are in a constant process of checking in with ourselves spiritually, mentally, and physically. Spend some quality time checking in with yourself about what is going on inside of you to get to the root of any feelings of misalignment.

It is like knowing when your parking meter is almost out of time and putting in a few more quarters before you get a ticket. Or, when your cell phone is losing bars, plugging it back in for a recharge before it dies.

Health educator Suzanne Sutton suggests that if you have been living out of alignment for too long, you may want to put yourself into radiance recovery intensive care mode for a while. Letting go of all that is stressful until you can reconnect with your radiant nature.

Take the responsibility for cultivating your foundation for radiance and bringing the elements into alignment. In the following sections we will learn how to live in harmony physically, mentally, and spiritually. With proper alignment through self-care, we gain clarity, stillness, and the ability to flow with whatever life brings with peace and wholeness.

We don't have to try to be more radiant; we are born with an abundance of beautiful light and energy. We only have to stop thinking and doing those things that keep us from connecting to our radiant nature. Become a radiance chiropractor and get yourself back into alignment.

Discovery Question:
What keeps me from taking care of myself?

30

Physical Alignment:

Taking Care of Our Radiant Body

"Happiness lies in the fulfillment of the spirit through the body."
~ Cyril Connolly

Our connection to our body gives us wisdom about what is going on in our lives. Our body naturally wants to be in alignment. That is why it gives us such obvious clues when we are off balance. Whatever is going on for us emotionally will show up in our bodies. If we get too stressed or upset, our bodies will react with tightness or illness. As we become more aware of what our body needs, we can take the steps needed to make our bodies happy.

Exercise

Our bodies were designed with the need to be physical as part of our survival. Today our culture has developed so many conveniences that we no longer have to use our body in the way it was intended. We have cars, washing machines, grocery stores, and running water. We run a vacuum instead of beating rugs, or turn on a heater instead of chopping wood. We take advantage of many other modern inventions that make life so much easier than it was for our ancestors, but often to the detriment of our physical bodies.

This being the case, we need to consciously create opportunities to use our joints and muscles to stay flexible, strong, and radiant. The practice of caring for our bodies translates into every part of our lives.

We have so many fun choices to keep our bodies radiant and healthy. Choose activities that will develop your strength, range of motion (flexibility), and aerobic capacity. It can be as simple as walking your dog or dancing in your living room. Maybe you love swimming or yoga. Perhaps it is time to take up hiking or Tai Chi, or join a gym. I just attended my friend Kimber's birthday bash where we had a blast playing with Hula-hoops.

Be creative and choose activities that you love because you are much more likely to do them than things you "should" do. If it gets your heart pumping and it is fun, it's exercise.

Sleep

Getting a regular good night of sleep of six to eight hours is so important, because that is our body's opportunity to renew. It is like turning off our computer and rebooting in the morning: We get a fresh start.

A Harvard study showed that with proper sleep we benefit our:

- Learning and memory,
- Metabolism and weight,
- Safety,
- Mood,
- Cardiovascular health, and
- Protection from disease.

Cherish a power nap. Find opportunities to take a nap during the day. For example, take the time that you might otherwise use to go for coffee and instead take a mid-day nap for renewal and energy.

Maintenance

Schedule regular visits with your doctor and dentist. This keeps your body and smile radiant, and gives you and the people who love you peace of mind.

Massage

Scheduling regular massage sessions will help you stay in much more than physical alignment. Massage also:

- Relieves stress, pain, and tension in your body,
- Improves circulation,
- Gives you time for renewal and self-care
- Allows you to practice receiving healing energy

Our bodies definitely want *all* of the above! There are so many types of massage, from Swedish to acupressure, Thai to reflexology. You can try different ones to see which your body responds best to. Massage schools offer budget-friendly options. It is important that, after exercising our muscles, we relax and care for them, too. While you are receiving your massage, you can visualize the therapist wringing out lactic acid and tension from your muscles, and let them go.

Posture

Our physical posture says a lot about how radiant we are. If we go around with our head hanging and shoulders forward, and with our heart protected and closed, our radiance can't shine. By letting our inner light lift our head, straighten our spine, and open our heart, we create a big, open window to our heart. Just try sitting or standing with your head down, arms crossed, body rounded and closed, then feel radiant. It's tough. Now, try lifting your head and putting your shoulders back and heart forward with a radiant smile, and feel the difference in your body.

With the foundation of exercise, sleep, and care, we make our bodies happy.

Discovery Questions:

How do I feel when I exercise my body?

What is enough exercise?
What is enough sleep?

Activities:
- Write down your favorite physical activities or sports. Which one(s) will you do today?
- Consciously set up a sleep schedule based upon what works best for you. Make a mid-day power nap part of it.
- Schedule your next check-up with your doctor and dentist.
- Schedule a massage.
- Be conscious of and improve your posture.

Gratitude:
Be grateful for all of the things your body can do.

Mantra:
I have a Radiant body!

Physical Alignment:

Radiant Nutrition

"We are indeed much more than what we eat, but what we eat can nevertheless help us to be much more than what we are."

~ Adelle Davis

Good nutrition is essential to maintaining a healthy body, and to help us sleep better, think better, slow down aging, combat illness, and cultivate radiance.

Consider what you put into your body. What energy is it creating? We have all had the experience of eating foods that make us feel lethargic or just yucky. In the Ayurvedic practice from India, the foods you eat are in alignment with your dosha, or body type. The belief is that certain foods can benefit or cause problems, depending on your dosha.

Our bodies feel strong and healthy when we eat natural foods.

In our modern culture there is an abundance of wheat, corn, sugar, fat, and chemical additives in processed foods. We consume far more than we realize. This is not what our bodies were designed to eat. Our bodies want fresh, live, local, seasonal, whole food that gives us light and energy. Give your body what it wants.

Kimber Simpkins, yoga master and author of *Finding Fullness*, has cut all sugar and most wheat out of her diet. She realized that it was not only affecting her body, but her mood as well. After playing with different combinations to find what makes her body most happy, she realized that she needs protein and vegetables for breakfast. It works!

Kathy Fettke, founder and CEO of Real Wealth Network, has cut caffeine, sugar, and alcohol out of her diet. She tells me it makes her nicer, which says a lot, because she is already an extremely nice person.

When we choose to put healthy foods into our body, we are reinforcing our beliefs about ourselves and what we feel we deserve.

If we were a high-performance car (choose your favorite), we would not put low-grade fuel into our tank, nor would we occasionally throw a handful of sugar into the tank; we know that we'd damage it. Be very conscious of what you are putting into your tank.

I have not eaten any meat for many years. As a vegetarian, I feel fantastic, lighter, and more radiant. Everyone has their own path, so it is about finding what works best for you and your fuel tank.

Not ready to go "cold turkey"? When it came to sugar, I wasn't either. That is mostly because I love sugar, especially in the form of chocolate. So, when I decided to cut back I started having "sugar-free" days. All of the odd days of the month (1st, 3rd, etc.) I do not eat any sugar. On even days I can have some if I'd like. It works for me because I am not depriving myself, and I have cut my intake by at least half. Someday I may go all the way, but for now this works for me. For you, it may be salt, fat, caffeine, or something else you know would make you healthier if you did less of. Then, find a way that works for you to move closer to your goal of physical alignment. This method can also work for time wasters, drains, or anything you are working to be free of.

We are free to eat whatever we want as long as we balance our desires (choices that *give* health and radiance), the amount of intake (no more than we *need*), and the ability to burn off at least as much as we've put in. Pretty simple. It's like the business model of "just in time delivery": We don't keep a stockpile (fat) in our body. We only need to have as much inventory as we are using.

If you haven't already, look into the "slow food" movement. They are educating people about the strong connection between their plate and the planet. When we are eating healthy, delicious food, it serves us to eat it slowly, breathe, and enjoy the flavors that nature provides us.

In the Buddhist practice of conscious eating, we eat in silence, and with each bite we contemplate gratitude for our food as well as the person or people who prepared it, bought it, sold it, shipped it, harvested it, grew it, planted it,and cultivated the land, plus all of their families and support systems. Our gratitude list could go on forever, but the main point is to be grateful for every bite. It is also important that we only take what we need and not throw anything away – to honor all of the energy that went into getting it to our plate. It is a wonderful way to get the maximum benefit from our food and cultivate radiance.

Give your body what it needs to be strong, balanced, healthy, and full of energy. You'll be more radiant before you know it!

Discovery Question:
What foods make me feel really good, and which ones make me feel crappy?

Activities:
- Play with some food combinations to find what works (or doesn't) for you.
- Make a list of your radiance foods.
- The next time you are shopping, instead of buying the "usual," consciously choose foods that will give your body maximum health benefits.
- To take it a step further, go to your pantry and donate

to a shelter anything that dims your light, Unless it is so unhealthy that you'd rather compost it.

- Practice eating meditation at one meal or snack each day for a week. Notice the difference of how you feel when you eat consciously, compared to how you feel when you mindlessly shovel food into your mouth.

Gratitude:
Be grateful for the abundance of fresh food available to you every day.

Mantra:
I create radiance with wholesome food.

32

Physical Alignment:

Honoring Our Environment

"Our environment is a reflection of our mind."
~ Jian Sheng Shifu

Our environment is a mirror that reflects what is going on inside us. We create the energy in our physical environment. This includes our home, car, office, and clothes, and the places we visit most. As you look around, is it what you want it to be? Just as certain people or situations can be drains or faucets, so can our physical environment.

We honor our environment by cleaning and clearing out clutter, organizing, and simplifying. As we consciously create our space, we align our external world with our internal world. Possibilities need space in order to grow into realities. In order to have spaciousness, we must rid ourselves of what no longer serves us.

Once we have created space, we can begin to create harmony.

We can decide what energy we want our home to hold. Are we looking for peace, inspiration, laughter, comfort, style, high energy, or a nurturing soft place to land? We can then choose the furniture, colors, textures, lighting, and art or photos that align with that intention. Maybe we would like a fountain or plants, soft bedding, fragrant aromas, more sunlight, or air flow. Outside, we may want the sound of wind chimes or the sight of garden beds filled with beautiful flowers to greet us. When creating, give attention to your senses: What is visually pleasing? What feels good, smells good, and sounds good?

Alison Marks, Feng Shui consultant and author of *The Little Book of Sanctuary*, offers her top three tools for creating alignment:

- Start with "Fresh Eyes." Go out to the street and come into your house as though you are seeing it for the first time. What do you experience? What kind of person lives here? What story does your home tell?
- Get really clear on three qualities you want for your home. It may be light-inspiration-comfort or serenity-warmth-freedom. Choose your three words and make them your mantra; base decisions on them. Rather than finding a random something and trying to figure out how it could fit in, look for specific items that align with what you want in our home.
- De-clutter. This one is pretty self-explanatory. Make room for what you want by getting rid of what you don't.

Our home is probably the most important space to honor since it is where so many important events happen in our lives. It can serve as our sanctuary. Use the same principles of cleanliness, organization, and comfort for your car and office.

Our environment also includes the clothes we wear. Depending on what we do all day, there may be certain expectations, but we can still do our best to be clean and comfortable. It may mean finding shoes that don't kill our feet, or wearing clothes that fit our body properly and align the way we look on the outside with who we are inside.

The places we visit regularly are also a reflection of what is going on inside. We want to spend as much time as possible in positive, energy-giving places and, obviously, less time in places that drain us. Take a look at the environments you consciously or unconsciously put yourself into. Are they in alignment with your radiant nature?

"There are two ways of spreading light: to be the candle or the mirror that reflects it."
~ Edith Wharton

All of our personal environments have the potential to be the radiant reflection of what is in our heart and mind. They don't have to be perfect, but we can make simple changes that honor our environment and bring us into the best possible alignment.

Discovery Question:
What environments give me physical energy?

Activities:
- Close your eyes for a few moments and visualize your radiance. Imagine what it will be like when your home, office, car, and clothing are reflecting your radiance. Get a sense in your body of how that will feel. What one thing could you do to start moving toward it?
- Make a list of energy faucets you could add to your environment.
- Now list energy drains that you will get rid of.
Choose at least one a day to implement.

Gratitude:
Appreciate the canvas you have on which to create your environment.

Mantra:
I create my environment from the inside.

Mental Alignment:

Being Fully Present

"In the present, every day is a miracle."

~ James G. Cozzens

Being engaged and present in our lives is important for fulfillment. We all want to feel good in our own skin, connected, mindful, and alive. We want to experience miracles.

Being fully present means that we are consciously connected to here and now in our body, mind, and heart. When all three are fully present, there is a certain stillness and ease because we only have to do one thing: be.

When we are present, we become aware of our thoughts. We notice whether they are contributing to our radiance and growth, or if we are stuck in the past. Perhaps we are out in the future and missing out on true connection. We've all heard the saying "The lights are on, but nobody's home." Without presence, our lights are not really on.

We may not even realize the mess we are getting ourselves into or how far out of alignment we have gotten. Our lives pass us by.

Presence, or lack thereof, sets the stage for how we perform.

One of the most infamous distractions to being fully present is being chased by our schedule. This is what it can look like:

> We wake up, and begin thinking about getting ready. While in the shower, we are thinking about what we will wear. While getting dressed, we think about what we are going to eat. As we eat we think about what needs to be done at work. While at work, we think about what we want to do on the weekend, and so on. We are never fully in the present – never being fulfilled; our mind is always somewhere else.

As my kids have gotten older they have made comments about me "not being there" when they were young. Granted, I did work a lot back then, but in my mind I had helped out in their classrooms, gone on every field trip, home-schooled, driven thousands of miles and been at countless activities, taken them traveling, and spent as much time with them as I could.

What I realized is that I wasn't really present with them. My mind was constantly on other things at work, or dwelling on something from the past, or anticipating the future. I wasn't really "there." I did the best I could to be present with the skills I had at the time, but it was time to change.

In my mid-20s, I read Dan Millman's book *The Way of the Peaceful Warrior*. His character Socrates asks, "Where are we?" and "What time is it?" The answers are always "here" and "now." This became my intention for my life.

I used to believe that I had a bad memory. Actually, I was wrong. My memory is good, but I had trouble remembering some things because my mind was somewhere else. Being this way left everyone unfulfilled, especially me. By not being present I had no connection to my radiant nature, and I made unconscious decisions or reacted from a mindless, egocentric place.

Today, I do my absolute best to be present in all of my tasks and relationships, especially the one with myself. It takes more energy at first, and I get less "stuff" done. The payoff is that while I'm focused on what I'm doing and who I am connecting with, my life is more fulfilling. My memory is also a lot better!

We must choose to be present in every moment, so it does take awareness on our part. The chances of "accidentally" being fully present are pretty slim. Give presence your attention, and make it your intention. Check in with your body, mind, and heart.

By becoming present so much more is available; we are free to play with many more possibilities, and able to make decisions from love and respond with kindness rather than old habits or an absent mind. Make presence a habit.

As we practice presence, our energy shifts from outside distractions to what we are feeling inside and we experience life in a new, radiant way.

Discovery Questions:
Who am I when I am fully present?
What is at stake when I am not present?

Activities:
- Practice becoming fully present in this moment, and the next, and the next... Strive for as many consecutive moments of presence as possible. Connect with the radiance around you. We must be engaged in order to keep up with the changes in life.
- Notice how your body feels when you are present.
- Notice what your impact on others is when you are fully present.
- Write down some things that help you to get present. Keep this list in your consciousness to help you become present at any moment.

Mantra:
I am here.

Mental Alignment:

Inspirational Input

"Without inspiration the best powers of the mind remain dormant, there is a fuel in us which needs to be ignited with sparks."
~ Johann Gottfried Von Herder

Our mind is unlimited, the only limits are put there by our way of thinking. What we put into our minds is like our mental juice. When we think good, dynamic, caring, and daring things, our minds are lubricated and they expand. Be aware of what you habitually put into your mind. Nourish and cultivate it with luscious, inspirational juices.

Read something encouraging every day. Keep your favorite books next to your bed and make inspirational reading part of your morning ritual. Whether we read just a sentence or an entire chapter, it is a wonderful way to get our mind warmed up for a day of positive thoughts. Ron and I enjoy taking turns reading to each other. Our shared perspectives inspire many conversations and deepen our understanding of the reading. We learn more about ourselves and, in turn, understand each other and our relationship better as well.

Watch movies and television programs that are uplifting, positive, loving, and encourage growth. Stay away from extreme violence, hate, or input that takes us out of mental alignment by encouraging negative thoughts.

Listen to music that speaks to your soul and gives you energy. Most of us have had the experience of music changing our mood and lifting our minds out of a funk. Recently, I had a difficult family situation to deal with and had to borrow a friend's car. When I turned on the car, "The Middle" by Jimmy Eat World was playing, and its lyrics told me "Everything, everything will be just fine. Everything, everything will be all right." Through tears I completely shifted my thoughts and was able to stop future tripping and get present with being "in the middle."

Kathy Fettke, investment expert, radio show host, and founder and CEO of The Real Wealth Network, is often exposed to negative or alarming information in her business. One of the tools she uses is to take in the information and appreciate it, and then she takes that knowledge and does something good with it. She creates radiance in her life and thousands of other lives as well.

"The most beautiful thing in the world is the conjunction of learning and inspiration."

~ Wanda Landowski

Explore different spiritual teachers. Check out Buddha, Jesus, Ghandi, Ram Das, Mohamed, Lao Tzu, Krishna, Martin Luther King, or anyone that you are curious about. Take what you like from their teachings, and leave the rest. Nobody has to be completely right or wrong. There are many good lessons that help us to gain a deeper understanding of ourselves and our connection to Source.

We have to be inspired and inspiring ourselves before we can share.

I.I.R.O. = Inspiration in, radiance out.

The most important inspirational input is what we say to ourselves. Author and speaker Jolie Barretta-Keyser looks into the mirror each day and unconditionally loves herself – not from a place of selfishness or narcissism, but from a deep love of who she really is. She feeds herself the input she needs to cultivate her own radiance, and then she shares it with the world.

Observe your own conversations. Listen to the energy in the way that you are speaking. Are you speaking from your radiant nature? What are the thoughts behind your conversations? Are you communicating with others who speak from their radiant nature? As we become more aware and conscious of our input, we will see a change in our output.

Discovery Question:
When I am conscious of only putting positive thoughts in my mind, how am I different?

Activities:
- Find several inspiring books and read from one each morning when you wake up for a week (or forever).
- Write down your criteria for the movies, TV, and music you will consume.
- Read a lesson from a spiritual teacher you would like to learn more about.
- Give yourself some inspirational juice. Look in the mirror and inspire yourself.
- Play with changing the energy of your conversations by being outrageously radiant and inviting the radiance of others out to play.

Gratitude:
Be grateful for all of the inspirational juice available, and drink in as much as you can.

Mantra:
I only put good things into my mind.

35

Mental Alignment:

Become an Olympic Learner

"Learning is the beginning of wealth. Learning is the beginning of health. Learning is the beginning of spirituality. Searching and learning is where the miracle process all begins."

~ *Jim Rohn*

Stimulating our minds cultivates radiance, and it's fun! Some people think that, at a certain age, they are too "old" or "set in their ways" to learn something new. Research has proven that our brains remain flexible throughout our entire lives, which means that we can go on learning, stretching, and growing!

I learn something new every day, unless I am careful.

There is always something new to learn. We learn not only for our own enrichment, but we learn so that we can share with others. There is a ripple effect because once we have learned something, we have changed, and how we relate to the world changes, too.

We can be very choosy about the place we live, the car we drive, the clothes we wear, or the food we eat, but we must be even choosier about what we choose to learn. As we know, what goes into our mind comes out as our actions.

Inspirational speaker and author Wes Hopper is very careful about the input of learning. He loves to study a variety of topics, go to classes, and read newsletters. He accumulates tons of enriching knowledge and then offers it as "Daily Gratitude," a free newsletter to educate and enlighten thousands of people every day. Wes avoids negative or discouraging people and messages, and it shows in the way he brings optimism and growth into "real" life through his writing.

"Say not, 'I have found the truth,' but rather, 'I have found a truth.'"
~ Kahlil Gibran

Beginner's Mind

When we believe that we are an "expert" we limit our ability to explore new possibilities. To learn from a beginner's mind, we let go of thinking we know, lower our arrogance, and honor our curiosity. We continue to look for the possibilities. Our mind becomes still and peaceful, and we go beyond the duality of extremes to discover our delusions and our mental habits to find many truths. Life is not black and white; it is not even gray. There is an entire spectrum of colors available to us all of the time. If we are too attached to something being exactly as we want it, serenity will elude us. The reality is that everything is in a state of change, and we must change our minds with it. Be ready to learn something new. Our heads are round so thoughts can change direction.

Get Curious

We live in a time where more information is readily available to us than ever before. With the Internet and communication systems we can learn about anything, anytime. There are myriad venues to get newsletters, blogs, or vlogs, or take classes, including on-line courses, webinars, and teleseminars. Many are free. Just start Googling what you are curious about. Then, share your curiosity with others to get fresh perspectives and to take your understanding to a new level.

Turn on your three pounds of genius.

Here are some brilliant ways to exercise and stimulate new pathways in our minds:

- Learn a new language.
- Take classes, or go to lectures or workshops.
- Travel to experience new environments and cultures.
- Do puzzles, solve riddles, and use your creative mind.
- Be daring. Try something that you've never done before.
- Develop your mind-body coordination by doing things on your opposite side. Eat, brush your teeth, draw, or use your mouse with your non-dominant hand. Step up or kick with your non-dominant leg. Talk about lowering your arrogance with a beginner's mind!
- Get physical. Use your body to stimulate the nerves and pump blood into your brain. Walk, take the stairs, try a new activity, and get your body learning, too.

Training our brain and becoming an Olympic learner align our mind. We experience more joy and fulfillment, and it makes us a more interesting and radiant person.

Discovery Question:
How am I different when I am stretching my mind?

Activity:
Create a list of ten to twenty things that you have always wanted to learn about. Choose one to start with, and, when you are ready, start another, and then another. It is a "working" list, so each time you find something else you are curious about, add it to the list.

Gratitude:
Appreciate your flexible and open mind.

Mantra:
There is no end to what I can learn.

Mental Alignment:

Taking Mental Break Days

"Inside myself is a place where I live all alone and that's where you renew your springs that never dry up."

~ Pearl Buck

As we live our lives as radiant super-humans, we'll all need to take a break at some point. Rather than waiting until our tank is empty, or we become ill, we can set aside special days to just take care of ourselves. In my work, with life and business coaching clients, this one tool makes a huge impact on their happiness. They go from feeling as though every day is never-ending and filled with stress, to having the freedom to take care of themselves and knowing how. Take a deep breath.

The Set-Up

Plan to take the day off of work. Get help with the kids and pets if needed. Let people know that you will be unavailable with an auto-response e-mail and voice-mail message. Unplug the T.V. Turn off your computer and phone.

Now what?

Really, anything you want! Be where you want to be, eat what you want to eat, and do what you want to do. It's *your* day, so you get to do what it takes to get yourself into alignment, but you *don't* get to feel a single ounce of guilt or spend time worrying about obligations.

Here are some suggestions from other radiant people:

- Schedule a spa day.
- Get out into nature. Go to the park, mountains, or nearest water.
- Curl up in bed or in a hammock with a good book or your favorite movies.
- Listen to your favorite music.
- Dance.
- Play.
- Meditate or take a day of silence.
- Take a nap.
- Get dirty. Do a project that gets you connected to the earth.
- Schedule a personal retreat at a renewal center.
- Get together with a close friend.
- Take a long walk.
- Take a creativity vacation and do a project.

Treat your day as a "personal retreat." One of my favorite personal retreats is to plan a day of hiking, meditating, and journaling in silence. I hike to one of my favorite spots in the hills, find a place to sit and meditate for 45 minutes to an hour, and then journal. Then I move on to another favorite spot and repeat. Sometimes I will spend some extra time just lying in the sun or having a snack. When I return after six hours or so, my mind is in a completely different place. I feel renewed.

You don't have to plan a long expensive trip to Hawaii (although that is a fabulous idea, too!); you can take a mental break day as often as you need. It will make you happier, more focused, and radiant.

Our special days are just that: special. But we can also take time for ourselves each day, spending quiet time alone. Even if you take only a few minutes, focus on recharging your battery and renewing your energy.

Discovery Question:
What recharges me?

Activities:
- Schedule a mental break day within two weeks of right now.
- Create your ideal mental break day.

Gratitude:
Appreciate the support you get from the people in your life that allows you to take a mental break day.

Mantra:
Taking a mental break day will keep me from having a mental breakdown.

Spiritual Alignment:

Giving

"Since you get more joy out of giving joy to others, you should put a good deal of thought into the happiness that you are able to give."
~ Eleanor Roosevelt

When I was an athlete, my coach, Barbara Fester, taught us that we have to give back all that we have taken from the sport of gymnastics. I took those words to heart and became a coach, judge, director, and gym owner. What I did not realize at the time is that, the more I gave to my passion, the more I would receive back, which left me ready to give more. It was a lovely cycle to get into.

Radiant people leave everyone and everything better than before; they rub off on life. When we give from our connection to Source there are so many ways to give that create radiant energy.

Words have wings, so speak good things.

Think of each word that you speak as a gift. Giving kind words or words of encouragement lets others feel seen and accepted. Everyone wants to be appreciated. As we create awareness around our own giving, we see more clearly all of the giving that is going on around us. Telling someone that he is doing a great job, thanking someone for excellent service, or acknowledging someone's talents and efforts lights her up.

Giving Our Compassion, Understanding, and Radiance

Giving emotional support to someone who needs it connects us with his radiance. That may look like simply listening or asking questions that will help him to escape deluded or critical thinking. Giving someone hope from our compassionate heart reminds him that he is not alone and that he will get through the tough times.

"The best way to find your self is to lose yourself in the service of others."   *~ Gandhi*

Giving Our Time in Service

I realized long ago that I do not actually work. I serve, and in doing so I give meaning to my life. The time I spend with friends, coaching clients, the women I sponsor, or doing volunteer work helps me to "walk my talk." It is impossible for me to advise or support others in doing what I am not doing myself. I've tried it; it doesn't work for me.

Serve from your radiant nature without obligation or expecting anything in return.

Be a Great Hugger

A really good hug can change someone's whole day. We all know how fantastic a hug feels, but hugging has many physiological advantages: Hugs increase hemoglobin blood counts, ease tension, build self esteem, let us know we are cared for and connected, and heal our heart. Get out there and do some hugging! Please, no fakey, wussy hugs – *real,* good ones.

Material Giving

Give material things that will make someone happy or more comfortable. Be generous with your giving. We have an abundance of things we can give to others. Practice giving away what you don't need. Sometimes we want to hold on to things in an attempt to gain security or validation. We must be willing to give away everything – even what we cherish the most.

I had a collection of shirts and uniforms from my gymnastic career. Many were from National, World, and Olympic competitions that I had coached or attended and dated back to the 80s. Each item had memories attached to it for me, but I felt like they would be of no value to anyone else. One day I decided that they were taking up space and I did not use them enough, so I bagged them up and took them down to Encore Gymnastics. I put them in the coaches' office with a sign telling them to take what they'd like. I came back a couple of days later thinking that I would have to re-bag them and take them to Goodwill. To my surprise all but a couple of items were gone. Those special mementos that I cherished were greatly appreciated by a new generation of coaches. My heart soared. Now, when I see someone wearing one of my shirts or team uniforms, I can tell them some stories that go with it. And, maybe they will pass it on.

More always shows up.

> There once was a generous and kind king. Everyone in the land loved him. People from all around would come to visit him and bring him the most beautiful and rare jewels. The king would graciously accept the gifts. But because the king was so happy and fulfilled, and had no attachment to material wealth, he was constantly giving away the jewels. It seemed like the more he gave away these precious jewels, the more people would give to him.

Our jewels may look like love, knowledge, skills, appreciation, our art, personal secrets, or time. There is no need to keep any of those things to yourself. The more you give away, the more you will receive.

The more I give from my heart, the more gets deposited into my happiness bank account – with interest!

Widen Your Giving Arms

When I teach creative movement to children we play lots of games. One of them is giving. We pretend to give a gift to the next dancer; it is a very focused, sweet, personal exchange of energy as they dance and pass on the imaginary gift. Then, we play with giving our gift to the world. The dancing gets much bigger: Their heads are lifted, and their arms open wide. They take their energy and spread it *way* beyond the limits of that space. The funny thing is that it does not make them tired; it actually creates more energy in the giver. We can consciously practice giving personal gifts and gifts to the world to create radiance.

We have more than enough to give when we are in alignment ourselves. Take care of yourself first, then share!

Discovery Questions:
What is the source of my giving?
What do I have to give?

Activities:
- Write down three new ways to practice giving each day for one week (or longer). Create a habit of generous giving by constantly looking for new ways to give.
- Start a giving journal. At the end of each day journal what you gave from your heart that day. Notice how easy it is to find opportunities to give.

Gratitude:
Appreciate that you have so much to give.

Mantra:
It is in my radiant nature to give.

Spiritual Alignment:

The Energy of Breath

"Breath is the place where the soul meets the body."

~ Greg Riley

Our breath is *the* most important element of radiance. No breath, no life. Fortunately, nature does not require us to be conscious to breathe, but much more is available to us when we are.

In an interview with Dennis Miu, Tai Chi and accupressure master, I asked him how he stayed so young and vibrant. He explained that when we are babies we breathe very deeply, expanding way down into our diaphragm. As we get older we start to breathe higher, into our chest. Ask a 10-year-old to take a deep breath and she will, most likely, expand her chest. When we are in our old age, our breath moves even higher, up into our throat, and each breath is shallower. Then, just before death, each breath is only in the mouth, until it leaves us entirely. Dennis trains himself to breathe deeply into his diaphragm, creating energy for his entire body.

We use our breath both consciously and unconsciously to return to an aligned state of being. Sadly, there are some people who live their entire lives without taking a conscious breath.

Greg Riley, Yoga master and coach, explains that breath is connected to our sympathetic and parasympathetic nervous systems. Think of our sympathetic nervous system as the reptilian "fight or flight" response, when cortisol and adrenaline get pumped into our system. Breathing becomes high in our chest, shallow, and unconscious. Our parasympathetic system is the flip side of the sympathetic; it is our "rest and relaxation" response. This is deep, calming breath, which uses the oxygen most effectively and efficiently, and releases the neurotransmitters that cause relaxation.

If we are feeling anxious, by simply becoming aware of our breathing and deepening our breath, we can re-align ourselves. It is very difficult to breathe deeply and be completely anxious at the same time. This is why we often see elite athletes taking deep breaths before they perform. They are giving their body what it wants: oxygen!

Our breath is also our connection to our radiant nature. When we understand the value of breath for connecting with our body, calming our mind, and expanding our awareness, we can use our breath as a tool to create radiance.

Discovery Question:
How will I use my breath to become more conscious and connected to my radiant nature?

Activity:
Try these simple techniques to get started on building your breath consciousness.

- Sit comfortably. Try sitting on the floor with your legs crossed or on a chair with your arms relaxed. The main thing is to be comfortable so that you will not be distracted by your body.
- Close your eyes and let go of any outside distractions. Focus on the air entering and leaving your nose. Feel the cool air come in and the warm air go out.
- Focus on breathing deeply. Direct your breath below your

navel. Take your breath deep into your abdomen without expanding your ribs first.

While breathing deeply, practice breath counting. Breathe in and out for the same number of counts: in-2-3-4, out-2-3-4. With practice you can build up your count, as long as you are not tense and do not force the breath. Keep it smooth.

Gratitude:
Be grateful for the times that breath has brought you into alignment.

Mantra:
I breathe deeply into my radiant nature.

Spiritual Alignment:

Clarity Through Meditation

"Meditation here may think down hours to moments. Here the heart may give a useful lesson to the head and learning wiser grow without his books."

~ *William Cowper*

If you don't have thirty minutes to meditate, you probably need an hour.

Sure, an hour would be nice, but we can spend a few minutes meditating and still get tremendous benefit. Sit quietly every day. Just sit and listen to your heart, release your mind, and let go of stress. You will extend your life and increase your inner peace and happiness. It will help you to resolve emotional misalignments such as fear, anxiety, obsession, depression, resentments, and you will improve your physical, mental, and spiritual health.

Meditation reduces stimulation from the outside world and allows our thoughts to settle down. Our minds are like a jar of dirty water: If we are constantly shaking it up it stays dirty, clouded with delusions and stress. If we set the jar down, after a while the dirt particles start to settle to the bottom and what we get at the top is clarity.

While meditation may look like just "sitting there doing nothing," it really is the fastest way to train our mind, to calm it down, and to clarify our thoughts. Until we become aware of our thoughts, we can't clean up our delusions and cultivate our radiance. We reflect inwardly to see our outside world with more clarity.

Through meditation we discipline our mind to be in the present moment. This is also a good time to be grateful and contemplate our blessings: the fact that you have a nice bed to wake up in, good clothes to wear, food to eat, and people who care about you. We can let go of any obstacles to our radiance and let our serenity shine.

The good news is that you can't fail at meditation. Any attempt is a success; any moment you spend with the intention of going inward and clearing your mind moves you forward. The aspiration is to create more consecutive moments of clarity.

When we meditate, we can explore our transcendental wisdom. To really understand transcendental wisdom, we must experience it. By calming our minds with daily practice, we will begin to understand. The results can be seen in our daily lives when we develop more patience, react less, and become more understanding, aware, and harmonized with our surroundings.

Our mediation practice frees our minds and opens space for more creativity, fulfillment, and higher thinking. It connects us to our Source and clears the "junk" from our mind so that our heart and body can respond to life without obstacles, allowing spiritual growth and healing.

Discovery Question:
What does clarity mean to me?

Activity:
There are several methods of meditation that we can use to begin our practice. Breath counting (see the previous section) and thought clearing are good ones to start with.
- Sit comfortably and begin to focus on your breathing.

- Begin to notice thoughts as they come up and let them settle to the bottom of the jar without attaching to them. You can also imagine your thoughts as passing clouds or as fluid that drains away, whatever serves you best.
- If you notice your mind drifting, take your awareness back to your breath.

You can start with sitting for just one minute every day, and build from there. Any time you being to feel physical or emotional stress you can use this tool to help you get centered and keep you from spiraling into an overwhelmed state. It is fun to do even when you are not stressed because you clear a path for your radiance.

It is a good idea to set your intentions for the day immediately after you meditate. The more benefit you see, the more motivated you will be to create space in your day for meditation.

Gratitude:
Appreciate the benefits of clarity.

Mantra:
I am not my thoughts; I am my radiant nature.

Element V: Vision

"Be daring, be different, be impractical, be anything that will assert integrity of purpose and imaginative vision against the play-it-safers, the creatures of the commonplace, the slaves of the ordinary." ~ Cecil Beaton

---

Radiance Vision

"Vision without action is merely a dream. Action without vision just passes the time. Vision with action can change the world."
~ *Joel A. Barker*

I have not yet found a way to take my body to the future but, through my mind, I can visualize my dreams.

We can type into our GPS where we are now and where we would like to go, and then be patient and open to the step-by-step directions to help us get there. The same goes for creating our radiance vision: As long as we keep moving and patiently holding the intention of our vision, we will stay on track. We create a blueprint or pathway to our dreams.

Our vision is about bringing it all together. See yourself living radiantly through integrating what you have learned from your beliefs, optimistic attitude, living with passion, and self-care alignment. Imagine what life will be like when this vision becomes reality.

Many of the greatest athletes visualize their performance as much as they practice physically. Have you ever seen an Olympic athlete get quiet, with his eyes closed and "in the zone" before his competition?

Olypmic athletes are trained to quiet all of the outside distractions, settle down their mind, and vividly visualize – in detail – how the performance will go. They are setting a strong mental intention in their mind first, and their body reacts to manifest it physically.

We can certainly do the same thing with our vision for our radiance plan. By quieting our minds, getting really clear on what we want, seeing it, and feeling it, we can create it in our lives. Our vision is unlimited and expansive. I am not suggesting that you can visualize something and it will automatically come true. Visualization is a tool to use in harmony with doing all of the right things. Olympians don't *just* visualize; they train really hard, too.

There is a beautiful, heart-opening pose in yoga that I really wanted to be able to do. For years I worked on it, but not diligently. It occurred to me that, while I talked about wanting to do the pose, I didn't act like it. So I began to visualize myself easily moving into the pose. When I practiced yoga in class or at home, I visualized my heart and hips opening. I did this for months. Then one day in class, my teacher used me as a demonstrator for that exact pose. I reached back for my foot and put it on my head easily. It felt just like I had visualized. I was thrilled. Of course, nobody else cared that I could do that, but I knew that my heart had opened, and I saw myself as a more open, loving person. If you want to be radiant, see yourself as radiant.

Vision is a prime motivator for our beliefs. When we see someone else do something, we believe that it can be done. That is one of the reasons why, in many of the sections in this book, we have been grateful for a role model for that lesson.

Read through the following sections, answering the discovery questions, and do the activities using imagination, insight, intuition, and contemplating what creates radiance in your life. Free yourself from limitations, and have fun playing with what feels good and all of the possibilities!

Setting Intentions

"We know there is intention and purpose in the universe, because there is intention and purpose in us."

~ *George Bernard Shaw*

Our vision can begin with setting intentions toward what gives life to our radiant nature. When you are thinking about what you want to create, it helps if it is something you can control, such as how you think, your perspective, or your attitude.

You may want to include these aspects from the previous chapters as part of your vision:

- **Self-acceptance:** What can I count on myself for?
- **Freedom of choice:** What choices must I make?
- **Empowerment:** What is my centered state?
- **Connection and intimacy:** How will I stay open-hearted, create deep connection, and keep the walls down?
- **Letting go:** What resentments or judgments (especially of myself) must I let go of?
- **Passion:** What makes me feel alive?
- **Vision:** How do I see my radiant self?

A lot of contemplation and many changes in our beliefs and attitudes are built into the foundation of what we want to create with our radiance plan. They are why we are doing it in the first place. When setting our intentions, it is best to keep it simple.

As we learned earlier, once we have an understanding of the "what" and the "why" of our dreams, the "how" becomes much more simple.

Discovery Questions:
What do I want to create more of in my life(e.g., peace, freedom, health, connection, serenity, intimacy, security)?
What am I activating inside myself?
What are my specific intentions for:
- a radiant body,
- a radiant mind,
- and a radiant spirit?

Activities:
- Write down your exciting, inspiring, and very specific intentions, and keep them in a place where you can see them every day.
- Speak your radiance intentions aloud daily. Give power to them through your words.
- Create your radiance plan. Start with your top intentions and brainstorm tactics you will use to obtain each intention. Establish three tactics for each intention.

Here is an example of what a radiance plan could look like:

Physical Radiance
1. Have a regular workout schedule. (intention)
   a. Strength, flexibility, and aerobic training as part of my morning ritual (tactic)
   b. Monday hike
   c. Thursday Yoga class
2. Only put healthy, nutritious food into my body. (intention)
   a. Go vegetarian one day a week

      b. Eat half as much sugar

      c. Shop at the farmer's market and cut out fast food

3. Get enough sleep. (intention)

      a. 8 hours per day, which may include a nap

      b. Comfortable bedding and environment

      c. Meditate 5 minutes before bed to clear my mind

Physical Radiance

1.

2.

3.

Mental Radiance

1.

2.

3.

Spiritual Radiance

1.

2.

3.

Go to www.TamaraGerlach.com for a PDF worksheet.

The Non-Negotiables

"The lives of happy people are dense with their own doings---crowded, active, thick. But the sorrowing are nomads, on a plane with few landmarks and no boundaries; sorrow's horizons are vague and it's demands are few."

~ Larry McMurtry

Radiant people maintain, as part of their self-care plan, certain things that are non-negotiable. These may include values and deeply held beliefs that are the foundation of success and that become part of the moral strategic plan. These are not demands that we make on the world, but rather guidelines that *we* live by – not expecting anyone else to share the same set of values.

Whether daily meditation, exercise, appreciation, or connecting with others or our Source, we all have things that keep us happy, centered, and in the flow of life. When we are being truly honest with ourselves about honoring our non-negotiables, we make our lives more aligned and radiant.

Patrick J. Ryan, author of *Awakened Wisdom: A Guide to Reclaiming Your Brilliance*, chooses "flexibility" as a non-negotiable. An excellent choice! By choosing to be flexible in every moment, he gives himself permission to play with spacious freedom. He is not locked into anything. As in the old saying "What doesn't bend, breaks," flexibility keeps Patrick from becoming rigid and breaking.

Consider your non-negotiables around these topics:

- Communication. Make a commitment about the way you will communicate with others. Are there words that you are just not willing to use? How will you allow people to communicate with you? What language or energy are you just unwilling to engage in?
- Self-care. Brushing your teeth, bathing, eating, and sleeping are givens, but also consider what will make your body, mind, and spirit really healthy. These may include exercise, journaling, or taking a nap.
- Values. Our values support all that we do. Your values may include respect, freedom, honesty, growth, or, like Patrick, flexibility. Think about which values are non-negotiable for you.
- Actions. These may include the way you live: committed to always serve the highest purpose and do your best. Or perhaps there are boundaries that you will not cross: cheating on your spouse, stealing, or intentionally harming another being.

Set an intention to live your life in such a way that you include uncompromised self-care that allows you to be fully you and to love yourself unconditionally.

Discovery Question:
What are my non-negotiables?

Activity:
Write down the *one* thing that you know you must do to cultivate radiance. Choose something that you are not doing right now, but that your spirit tells you would feel good.

Gratitude:
Appreciate a person who has taught you about values and morals, and who walks her talk.

Mantra:
I stand in integrity with courage and discipline.

Innovation and Creativity

"Creativity is a drug I cannot live without."

~Cecil B. DeMille

We know how to find inspiration in others and everything around us; we can also find inspiration in ourselves. Our intuition is powerful enough to guide us into what needs to be created next. Begin to receive raw information from your environment and your body, without allowing your head to attach any meaning to it; just feel it.

Be daring in your creativity. My level of fulfillment is directly related to my level of daring. I *need* to be creating at all times. It is my nature, and I believe that it is everyone's nature.

"If you limit your choices only to what seems possible or reasonable, you disconnect yourself from what you truly want, and all that is left is a compromise."

~ Robert Fritz

Create pictures of your future. Let your mind completely relax and be free, and then play with seeing all of the things that you can and will do when you are living your radiance plan, empowered, healthy, and full of energy. Whether it is learning a new skill, or taking that trip you have always dreamed of, or walking into a crowded room, or speaking to a large group with confidence and serenity, rather than putting it into words, create pictures in your mind.

Play with the possibilities and your preferences. Notice that we are not using "expectations." Setting expectations is a sure sign that you will be disappointed. When we express preferences, we might like something to be a certain way, but are not attached to it and leave potential for *way* more than our little minds could have imagined.

The details of your radiance plan are unique to you. It does not matter what anyone else thinks; the transformation starts with you, your creativity, your growth, your thoughts, and your feelings.

An excellent sign that you are being daring in your creativity is when people are saying that you are being ridiculous, absurd, crazy, eccentric, unreasonable, or wacky. Start hanging out with the people who are willing to play there with you. Later, you will be praised for your originality, talent, vision, brilliance, and imagination.

Turn on your creativity! Embrace your creative talents; it feels good, and the time is now. Waiting for the right circumstances to create your dream life is like waiting to have sex in your old age. Why would you do that?! Wake up your muse and shake up your life!

Discovery Question:
What is the story of my life one year from now?

Activity:
Work out your creativity muscles and get the creative juices flowing into your radiance plan. Twist, stretch, bend, move! Here are some fun ways:
- Look at things differently. Change your perspective, seeing things from all sides, upside-down, and with your eyes closed.
- Get old ideas out of your head to make room for new ones.

Practice with a beginner's mind.

- Reverse your assumptions. What if the *opposite* of what you believe to be true was reality?
- Notice what others have missed. See the details *and* the "big picture".
- Get curious. What else is possible?
- Create beyond your perceived capabilities and grow into it. What would stretch you? What would feel daring? What serves your desire?
- Develop a creative project – something that you are passionate about: making jewelry, writing a book, building a boat, etc. Find ways to make creativity a part of your daily life.
- Try something new every day. Grow, in ways big or small. What is one "average" thing in your life that you could love into greatness today?
- Create from everything. What inspires you? From where you are sitting right now, find ten things that inspire creativity in you.

Gratitude:
Appreciate your own creativity as well as everyone and everything around you that inspires you.

Mantra:
I am the writer of my own story.

Choreographing Your Radiance Plan

"Beauty is a radiance that originates from within and comes from inner security and strong character."

~ *Jane Seymour*

We have made a number of discoveries and deepened our understanding of ourselves, but simply knowing is not enough. It is time to put our new awareness into action! When we align our beliefs, attitudes, passions, and actions, we create energy for the manifestation of our vision.

It is easy to be seen as radiant if others around you are among the "walking dead." Who would you have to be, and how would you have to step it up, if you lived in a world where everyone was connected to their radiant source and lived creative, joyful lives? Design your plan to play the big game.

As a choreographer I've learned that there are so many components to consider when putting together a one-and-a-half-minute gymnastics routine. Below are a few that will translate into your radiance plan:

- Theme. Create a theme for each day or week. Your theme will give you a fundamental component and unify your plan. For example: "Today my theme is cultivating compassion" or "This week my theme is connecting with nature."

- Tempo. You do not want to create something with a slow, boring, and monotonous rhythm. Do what makes you come alive at times and what helps you to get centered at other times.
- Elements. Build into your plan the elements that help you to center and align, as well as special care elements like getting massages, trips to the spa, or "me" time. Do things that align with your purpose.
- Connections and transitions. Create a flow from one form of self-care to another. Rather than turning our self-care on and off like a switch, so that we only care for ourselves when it's convenient and all of our other responsibilities are fulfilled, or jumping in and out of radiance, we can bring self-care into everything we do with intention and clarity.
- Attainability. Constantly cultivate yourself. If you are never afraid, then you are merely living in your comfort zone; you're not really stretching or becoming fully alive. Create a plan that constantly pushes you to grow and also feels good. If it is too difficult, you'll be anxious or overwhelmed, and if it is too easy, you'll get bored. Find "enough."
- Fun and entertainment. Do what you love; entertain yourself. Create a radiance plan that is fun and inspiring, and make it a priority in your life. Dream of a big pay-off. Make these the most enjoyable hours of your day. Why not make it your *whole* day?

Seduce yourself into practicing your plan. Do what makes you feel really good. Don't worry about what you "should" do. Start with your non-negotiables, and add in what you want to do. Finding the joy in self-care.

Cut out any and all excuses. If you are using "not enough time" as an excuse to keep yourself from cultivating your radiance, consider who does your scheduling. You wouldn't forget to shower, brush your teeth, or eat. You might begin by giving yourself five minutes of self-care. You can work your way up to more time as you begin to see the positive results you are creating.

A Radiant Start to Your Day

Many of the people I interviewed have built self-care into their morning ritual. Time that they take each morning to set their intention, and to care for themselves physically, mentally, and spiritually, gives them a head start on a radiant day.

Rich Fettke is the author of *Extreme Success*. Along with yoga, meditation, and a gratitude ceremony, he has a practice of doing his age times ten worth of push-ups, pull-ups, and sit-ups every day as part of his morning ritual. Every year he just keeps getting better!

Remember that you have all of the strength, passion, and internal resources you need. When you receive the benefits of a little self-care, you will be inspired to do more.

Your radiance plan must have your own unique flavor in order for you to live it authentically. Sometimes it takes some experimentation to find what works for you. Please, don't give up on yourself.

As you create new habits, remember:
- Repetition is key.
- Be diligent.
- Be patience.
- Have good motivation.
- Know your "why."

The simplest changes may have the greatest impact.

Imagine simply meditating every day for only fifteen minutes. That is more than seven hours per month, and ninety-one hours per year! Think you how serene you could be! Twenty minutes per day would get you almost 122 hours of serenity per year!

Native Americans share the stories about teaching a child to jump over a corn stalk. The child doesn't start by jumping five feet in the air; he starts when the corn stalk is small and continues to leap over it every day. The moral is that we learn to do seemingly impossible things a little at a time by practicing every day.

It can feel a little, or a lot, overwhelming at first. Of course, you don't have to do everything on your dream list every day. Choose one or two "big" things to do from your list each month. By the end of one year, you will have done a lot!

Listen to what you need right now. You can always change it later.

You don't have to establish a strict routine. Doing the same thing day after day, week after week, or month after month sounds horribly boring to most creative, innovative people. Instead, create a whole menu of things to choose from each day that will satisfy your priorities. Add to your lists when you are inspired (which could be every day!).

Here are some examples to get you started:
- Choose several inspirational books to read from each day.
- Think of ten different ways to get a cardio workout.
- Practice new ways of giving.
- Choose things from your "Olympic learner" list.
- Make a list of the important relationships you want to nurture.

The most important thing is to remember to find ways to make cultivating radiance fun and challenging. If something is not giving you juice, it will not last long. But, be efficient with your time. Choose things from your menu that fit with a particular day. If you will have a lot of physical work that day, you may want to cut back on exercise. If you will have a lot of mental work, a little more meditation and exercise may serve you best.

Based on what you do for a living and what you have available, you can create your own challenges from everything. For example, when I have to stay in a hotel room, I just use the furniture as my workout gym or walk the halls. There's no need to drop our plan; we can adapt to any situation. A bed makes a great trampoline, no matter what Mom said!

There are no shortcuts to cultivating radiance. Although it may seem a little much at first, create your plan, and stick to it for thirty days so that you can start to create habits. When self-care comes easily and naturally to you, you can let go of the format.

The change happens on all levels: physical, mental, and spiritual. Shifting what you believe is vital. If you believe that you *are* your new habits, they will be much easier to achieve.

Life decisions can be made based on your radiance plan. If it fits, do it; if not, don't – or change your plan. This is a working plan and must change as the flow of your world changes, so use your intuition and wisdom when making changes.

You also don't get to beat yourself up. This is about self-*care* and compassion. Accept *complete* responsibility for your radiance plan. No excuses; no way that anybody or anything can make you quit; no complaining. *You* are responsible. Be *all in*; give yourself to your plan completely. You don't get to reschedule your mental, physical, and spiritual health.

Mostly, HAVE FUN!!! Love your radiance plan. It's your life!

Discovery Questions:
What does it mean to be "all in"?
What external resources will I need to gather (e.g., yoga mat, tennis shoes, journal, candles, space)?
What internal resources will I need to cultivate (e.g., patience, diligence, creativity, confidence)?

Activities:
- Design a five-minute to one-hour "morning ritual" based upon what fits into your life right now. It's okay if it is not the morning. Find time and begin doing it today!
- Create a checklist or chart of your intentions:
  - Daily and weekly habits that you will cultivate,
  - Time lines – start with this month, and

- Accountability (team support).
- Celebrate your success and then flow into your next intention.
- Daily journal check in. Each morning ask:
  - How do I feel today?
  - What is my intention for today? Invoke your radiance super-powers.
  - What worked yesterday?
  - What was challenging?
  - How will I care for and stretch myself today?
  - What would stir my soul today? Do that.

Gratitude:
Appreciate the time you have dedicated to your self-care.

Mantra:
I choreograph the dance of my life.

Creating Your Team:
Who Will You Invite to the Party?

"Man's best support is a very dear friend."

~ Marcus Tullius Cicero

Creating a "family" or team of people who support us is vital to our success. Be they tribes, sanghas, or villages, throughout time cultures have created support systems.

These days many of us grew up without a sense of community, or have disconnected ourselves as adults. We are told to "be independent," "stand on our own," or "figure it out" ourselves. How many times have you heard "Don't come to me with problems; bring me solutions"? If we had the solution, it would not be a problem! It is time for us to let go of our old beliefs that require us to do everything alone.

The world is made up of teams of people who work together for a common goal. Imagine if you were determined to win a soccer tournament. Everyone else came with a team, but you figured you could do it on your own. Fat chance you would make it past the first game! Why do we think we can go it alone in other aspects of our lives?

Some of us are so used to taking care of others and over-giving that it may be difficult to receive. We would rather do it ourselves and not "bother" anyone. That is why creating a team is so important; we don't have to go to any one person for everything. We can share different things with different people, giving them an opportunity to offer their "super-powers" to us and to feel "well used."

This is not a one-way street. As a generous giver, you know how good it feels to contribute to someone else's success and to have a positive impact. Don't hold that back from others; that would be ripping them off of the pleasure of being part of your life. You are too amazing not to share yourself with the world!

We need others for support, inspiration, and perspective. We benefit from a variety of perspectives, wisdom, and knowledge, and also deepen our connections to the important people in our lives.

Choose friends and family who are positive, who will hold you accountable, and who will celebrate with you. Choose people whose strengths complement your challenges.

> There is an old Buddhist story about two groups of people who have died. For eternity they are given as much delicious food as they want, but they have long chopsticks attached to the ends of their hands. The chopsticks are so long that there is no way to maneuver the food into their own mouths. While one group lives in Hell, desperately trying to get the fabulous food on the table into their mouths, failing, angry, and starving, the other group lives in Heaven, kindly feeding each other the bountiful feast.

Are you in Heaven or Hell?
Do you try to do everything yourself?
Do you serve others and let them serve you?

Life is a team sport the more carefully you choose your team, the better you play. Choose radiant people who:
- Are into growth and share in your thinking,
- Adore and accept you as you are,

- Have an outrageously optimistic attitude,
- Will hold you accountable,
- Will celebrate with you, and
- Possess strengths that complement your challenges.

Consider the relationships that you would like to nurture with your family, children, friends, acquaintances, co-workers, and elders. You may also want to work with a professional life coach or therapist. Perhaps you will want to include on-line support through a social media site or a blog.

Share your vision and goals with your team. Talk with them regularly to build energy and get support, but remember: *You* are responsible for your own self-care and cultivating your own radiance.

Discovery Question:
Who is on my team?

Activities:

- List each person's strengths and how they complement yours.
- Tell the members of your team about your plan and ask each which parts they would like to help with. You may discover talents that you did not know about.

Gratitude:
Appreciate the people who are willing to share their gifts, inspire, and support you.

Mantra:
When I ask, I have all the support I need.

A Radiant Front Row

Below is a poem that I found years ago that speaks to "Faucets and Drains" and "Creating Your Team." Enjoy. (The author is unknown.)

Not everyone can have a front row seat.

Life is a theater so invite your audiences carefully.

Not everyone is holy enough and healthy enough to have a FRONT ROW seat in our lives. There are some people in your life who need to be loved from a distance. It's amazing what you can accomplish when you let go, or at least minimize your time with draining, negative, incompatible, not-going-anywhere relationships, friendships, and family!

Not everyone can be in your FRONT ROW.

Observe the relationships around you. Pay attention to: Which ones lift and which ones lean? Which ones encourage, and which ones discourage? Which ones are on a path of growth uphill and which ones are just going downhill? When you leave certain people, do you feel better or feel worse? Which ones always have drama or don't really understand, know and appreciate you, and the gift that lies within you?

Not everyone can be in your FRONT ROW.

The more you seek God and the things of God, the more you seek quality; the more you seek not just the hand of God, but the face of God, the more you seek things honorable; the more you seek growth, peace of mind, love, and truth around you, the easier it will become for you to decide who gets to sit in the FRONT ROW and who should be moved to the balcony of your life.

Everyone can't be in your FRONT ROW.

You cannot change the people around you...but you can change the people you are around! Ask God for wisdom and discernment and choose wisely the people who sit in the FRONT ROW of your life. Remember the FRONT ROW seats are for special and deserving people and those who sit in your FRONT ROW should be chosen carefully.

Everyone can't be in your FRONT ROW.

Discovery Question:
Who belongs in my front row?

Activity:
Ask them for support in what you are doing.

Gratitude:
Appreciate Source for appearing through the radiant people in your life.

Mantra:
My "front row" is radiant!

Conclusion

Do you remember Grace, the young girl you met in the Introduction? Today, our radiant Grace believes in herself and is connected to her Source. She sees the beauty in everything and everyone, especially herself, and has realized that developing her inner light is better than any cosmetics. She lives a life of passion and purpose, listening to her heart and speaking her truth with confidence and compassion.

Our fabulous Grace has learned that it is simple to take care of herself in a way that is both nurturing and loving to her, and respectful to the people around her, creating more deeply loving and fulfilling relationships than she could ever have imagined. She effortlessly and playfully shares her light and joy with everyone around her, and her heart is a magnet for love.

Grace understands that by patiently and diligently continuing on this path of becoming fully present and accepting who she is becoming, she will experience more and more freedom and she'll slip less and less into old patterns that put her serenity at stake. She enthusiastically accepts and appreciates her blessings and sees her life as an adventure, with one delightful surprise after another. Grace's life keeps getting better – and she is just getting started.

Radiance Wheel

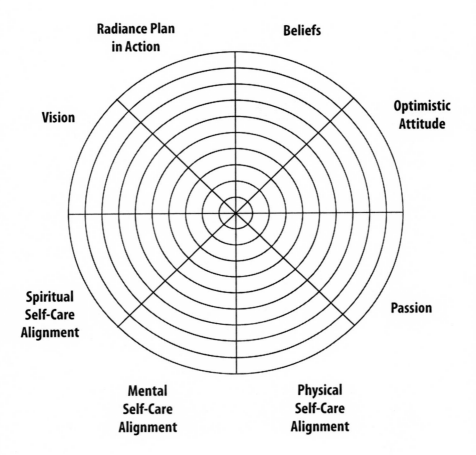

Radiance Plan in Action

Beliefs

Optimistic Attitude

Vision

Spiritual Self-Care Alignment

Passion

Mental Self-Care Alignment

Physical Self-Care Alignment

The Radiance Wheel is an excellent tool for tracking how radiant you feel at any time. It can be done on this fancy chart, or you can re-draw it on a napkin or in the sand. Mainly, it is useful to check in with yourself so you can celebrate your self-care or shift your energy as needed.

How to use the Radiance Wheel:

- On a scale of 0 to 10, how fulfilled are you in each of the categories on the Radiance Wheel? Zero means "non-existent" at the center, and 10, on the outer circle, means "extremely high."
- Rate each section, darkening the line where your score would be on the scale.

Remember: It is about how *you* feel in this moment; not in the past or planned for the future, but now. Go with your first impression without taking time to justify how it could be different. In other words, keep your mind out of it and let your heart do the work.

- Go around the wheel by answering these questions or others that help you clarify your Radiance:
  - Are your beliefs serving your life right now? Are you open-minded, accepting, and plugged into your Source?
  - Do you have an optimistic attitude? Are you being playful, joyful, and flexible?
  - Are you living with passion, dreams, and purpose?
  - Are you taking care of your body and environment?
  - Are you being mindful, being present, and stretching yourself?
  - Is your spiritual connection strong?
  - Do you have a clear vision of what you want for your life?
  - Are you living and expanding your radiance plan?

Once you have given each radiance category a number and darkened the corresponding line, take a look at how balanced your wheel is. If it truly was a wheel, how well would it roll?

- Write down what a 10 is for each category. It is important to know what a 10 is in order to move toward it. It becomes like a magnet that is constantly drawing you closer.

- Next, for each category, choose one thing that would bring your score up by at least one point. Then do it. Consciously take actions that will continue to move you toward your 10.

You can update this as often as you'd like. As you progress, your 10 will change, just keep moving toward it. Just don't do anything to move back toward a 1.

Download the PDF from www.TamaraGerlach.com.

Beliefs
Where I am now? _____ (Fill in the number.) Why?

What is a 10?

How will I move closer to my 10?

Optimistic Attitude
Where I am now? _____ Why?

What is a 10?

How will I move closer to my 10?

Passion
Where I am now? _____ Why?

What is a 10?

How will I move closer to my 10?

Physical Self-Care Alignment
Where I am now? _____ Why?

What is a 10?

How will I move closer to my 10?

Mental Self-Care Alignment
Where I am now? _____ Why?

What is a 10?

How will I move closer to my 10?

Spiritual Self-Care Alignment
Where I am now? _____ Why?

What is a 10?

How will I move closer to my 10?

Vision
Where I am now? _____ Why?

What is a 10?

How will I move closer to my 10?

Radiance Plan in Action
Where I am now? _____ Why?

What is a 10?

How will I move closer to my 10?

R.A.D.I.A.N.C.E.

You can use this simple acronym to remind yourself of your Radiance. It can be spoken as a daily mantra or posted as a visual reminder. You can also create your own with words that resonate with you. I would love to hear other possibilities that you come up with. Please contact me if you would like to inspire others by sharing your brilliance.

Reflect. I reflect the beauty, gifts, and love that live inside me and the beauty, gifts, and love I see in you.

Appreciate. I am aware of the abundance available to me and appreciate all the gifts life offers.

Dare. I dare myself to create, innovate, and live my life with courage. I speak my truth and dare to dream.

Inspire. I breathe life into everything I do and wake willing souls by just being me.

Accept. I accept myself as I am, you as you are, and life as it is. I accept adversity as my teacher and I accept responsibility for the radiance in my life.

Notice. I am aware and mindful about what is present in my mind, body, heart and environment. I notice when I am out of alignment.

Connect. I am connected to my Source, my heart, and you. I express myself clearly and with authenticity when I am connected.

Evolve. I am flexible, adaptive, and able to let go of the past to step into the possibilities of a radiant future. I cultivate the wholeness of my being.

(Go to tamaragerlach.com for a color PDF)

Radiance Is...

Radiance is...

Empowerment
Compassion
Optimism
A Bright Smile
Energized
Giving
Alignment
Connectedness
Accepting
Appreciation
Patience
Inspiration
Flexibility
Health
Creativity
Passion
Presence
Enlightened
Joy
Confidence
Honesty
Integrity
Contentment
Focused
Whole
Supportive

Radiance is not...

Victimization
Judgment
A Bomber Attitude
Avoidance
Exhaustion
Selfishness
Frazzled
Neglected
Critical
Taking for Granted
Frustration
Stuck
Stubbornness
Spiritually and Physically Sick
Dull and Boring
Apathy
Unaware
Ignorance
Resentfulness
Undermining
Delusion
Demoralization
Wanting
Confusion
Fragmented
Uselessness

Resources:

To find more information on cultivating your radiance visit the websites of these great authors, teachers, coaches, and radiant people.

Rich Fettke – www.Fettke.com

Patrick J. Ryan – www.AwakenedWisdom.com

Kathy Fettke – www.RealWealthNetwork.com

Kristine Carlson – www.KristineCarlson.com

Kimber Simpkins – www.Kimberyoga.com

Greg Riley – www.upwardspiralyoga.com

Wes Hopper – www.dailygratitude.com

Francine Allaire – www.thedaringwoman.com

Mai Vu – www.maivucoach.com

Dan Millman – www.danmillman.com

Jolie Barretta-Keyser – www.ecdspaces.com

Alison Marks – www.fromcluttertoorder.com

Kelli Wilson – www.asimpleplanconsulting.com

Virginia Kelley – www.EncoreGym.com

Tara Brach – www.tarabrach.com

Marci Shimoff – www.marcishimoff.com

Sue Walden – www.improvworks.org

Robin Sharma – www.RobinSharma.com

Lisa Elfstrum – www.lisaandcompany.com

Steve Zodtner – www.usli.com

Ron Abram – www.Abraminterstate.com

May you honor your inner teacher,
May you benefit from the knowledge and
understanding you have gained from this book,
And may you delight in the experience of
cultivating radiance!

About the
Author

Tamara has taught, mentored, and coached thousands of people to create freedom and cultivate their radiance since 1982. Tam brings her light, spirituality, creativity, and experience as an entrepreneur, author, speaker, wife, mother, Buddhist, yogini, and a life and business coaching to everything she does. She is all about creating opportunities for others to deeply experience what they are learning, and loves to inspire others to become empowered and to get into action around changing their lives. And the more fun they can have doing it, the better!

Tamara bought her first business, Encore Gymnastics, Dance and Climbing, in 1989. A former National Team Coach for USA Gymnastics, Junior Olympic Program Committee Member, and member of the Board of Directors, she has been involved in sports as a competitive athlete, coach, choreographer, and judge.

She began Prana Life and Business coaching in 2001 after working with Rich Fettke for several years and seeing the impact coaches have on people and businesses. She obtained her training through the Coaches Training Institute, as well as completing leadership training through Coactive Space. She has assisted numerous courses and a leadership course.

She is passionate about working with business leaders, entrepreneurs, athletes, parents, students, and anyone who wants to empower their life.

She had made olives with her father over the years, so in 2006 she opened Gerlach Olives and Oil. She finds joy in sharing her delicious creations with others.

Tam is a woman who follows her passions to fulfill her purpose in all aspects of her life. She lives on a ranch in the San Francisco Bay Area with her partner, Ron, and son, Kyle.

You can contact Tam at:
www.TamaraGerlach.com
Tam@TamaraGerlach.com
(925) 864–2093

CPSIA information can be obtained at www.ICGtesting.com
Printed in the USA
BVOW070127031011

272658BV00001B/58/P